women on the verge of societal breakdown

SAB

Sustainable
Autonomous
Base

EDC

Every
Day
Carry

Women on the Verge of Societal Breakdown

Preserving Hard-Won Freedoms during an Age of Uncertainty

Piero San Giorgio

Women on the Verge of Societal Breakdown:
Preserving Hard-Won Freedoms
during an Age of Uncertainty

Original title: *Femmes au bord de la crise*
English translation by Dmitry Orlov

© 2014 Piero San Giorgio

Original cover art by Matt Harter,
inspired by the art of Fan Ho

Publication date: November 1, 2016

ISBN-13: 978-1539160328
ISBN-10: 1539160327

Club Orlov Press
http://ClubOrlovPress.blogspot.com
cluborlovpress@gmail.com

Contents

Foreword to the French Edition

As soon as she gives birth, a woman says good-bye to a care-free life. She has to get up a dozen times every night, to make sure that her infant is breathing and didn't toss off the blanket, and to nurse it... She surprises herself that she performed the miracle of creating a new life, but all of her actions are so natural... The skill in taking care of a newborn child is part of a woman's DNA. This does not mean that fathers love their children any less. They just love them differently... No doubt, this is explained by the fact that male genes preserve the memory of the millions of years of hunt and battle, which were necessary to feed and defend their families.

This relates to virtually all species of animals. All you have to do is look at nature. The females instinctively fulfill the needs and wants of their offspring. They feed them, keep them warm, teach them to walk, swim, fly and defend themselves against predators, at once patient and demanding.

No matter how paradoxical this seems, but it was thanks specifically to Piero San Giorgio that I realized something essential: it would appear that we humans—the only species thought to be endowed with reason—have several decades ago forgotten the examples and the lessons of our fathers and mothers, and have embraced the idea that we should entrust everything to strangers, be it feeding our children, caring for their health, their upbringing, their defense, responsibility, values, common sense... all of this without even making sure that these strangers are worthy of our trust!

But now we know that they are not. We needed time, and the public scandals, for the light to shine on the corruption, the unfairness, the criminality—all plain to see in cases such as the asbestos industry[1] and the Mediator,[2] etc.—in order to reach the conclusion that the world is ruled by psychopathic money-printers who are ready to do anything for a bit of extra profit. These people are the ones who pull the strings of the puppets who, in turn, rule us, and entirely neglect the human beings they have ensnared in their nets. For them, a living human being is just a patent commodity.

They abominably mistreat animals.

They destroy all that is beautiful or beneficial that is given to us by nature to fulfill our vital needs.

They poison trees, soil, insects, bees, oceans, fish, the vegetables we eat, rivers, the waters of springs and the air we breathe.

They use fear and lies to inject our children with vaccines whose benefit they have never been able to prove, and they

---

1 *Global conspiracy against health* (*Complot mondial contre la santé*)
2 *Food is the Best Medicine* (*Les aliments sont les meilleurs médicaments*)

2

refuse to take into account the dangers and the consequences, which can make our children invalids for life...

They take advantage of the "economic crisis" in order to make the noose around our necks tighter and tighter...

They do everything to make us dependent, to lower us to the position of slaves, to push us to swallow their poison until we die, to make us take part—whether voluntarily or forcibly— in their villainous wars, and the endless suffering caused by their chemical and bacteriological weapons.

But what is our role in all of this?

Through ignorance, through passivity or cowardice, we condone them. It is as if we had gone blind, and now every-thing is in their hands.

Never before has humanity been under such an all-encom-passing, global attack. Never before has it been so difficult to protect our children. Based on the forecasts from the French Institute for Medical Oversight,[3] in the near future one child out of 440 will develop cancer before reaching the age of 15, and half of these before the age of five. One of every 80 chil-dren (and one of every 56 boys) is autistic. But never in the history of the world have children been so cared for, or re-ceived so many vaccines and drugs. It is absurd to suggest that such figures are in any way connected with the increase in av-erage life expectancy! Oncological, chronic and autoimmune diseases flourish, while at the same time television spreads in-formational fables while suppressing information about irre-versible contamination connected, in particular, with geneti-cally modified organisms and pesticides!

---

3 *Enough! Our children are more important than the CAC 40* (La coupe est pleine : Nos enfants sont plus précieux que le CAC 40)

3

In some countries, public debt has reached 95 to 200 percent of GDP, while poverty is spreading around our planet at full gallop... How can this debt ever be repaid? It is not accidental that throughout the world we are being deprived of our right to plant our own crops, to cultivate our own gardens: this is the best proof that they are doing this not to combat poverty but for the sake of profit. It is enough to take a look at India, Africa, and now also at Colombia, in order to understand what will occur in Europe in the near future once the latest transatlantic trade treaties have been signed...

Are we to live and to suffer, like the multitudes who allowed themselves to be herded into concentration camps, because they refused to believe that such nightmares were possible? There is nothing good to be expected of these people. They have no conscience, and life has no value to them. At least, not our life.

Anything that is good can only come from our own selves. We have to learn to say "No!"—to never again believe what the "authoritative" sources in mass media tell us, to disregard the propaganda, and to fight against those who are killing us... I personally believe that this would already be a big step forward!

We must give credit to Piero San Giorgio, whose previous books *Survive Economic Collapse*[4] and *Mean Streets* (*Rues Barbares*, co-authored with Vol West), have shaken us out of our stupor. Yes, the prognosis is dire, and we must become the owners of our lives, defend ourselves, take care of each other, organize... He gave us the keys, the ideas, the solutions, the projects, things to do to prepare, so that we don't end up like drowning

4 *Survive the Economic Collapse*, Radix Editions, USA; 2014.

rats the day it will all inevitably unravel. It is particularly important that he addresses his new book directly to women.

Men tend to see things at a large scale. They can carry heavy bags, split entire chords of wood. But it is the women who are the Guardians of the Temple. They are the ones who take care of the small details, who know about all the specific needs of the family. It is they who think about buying needles and thread, bandages and dehydrated garlic, unchlorinated water and Arnica cream,[5] who check the expiration dates on packages...

We, the ones whom our mothers told: "Work! Don't depend on your husband!" must now combine domestic work with bringing up our children, all the while remaining feminine and keeping our marriages alive... Obviously, we did gain a certain amount of independence, but too many men take advantage of it to stay on the sidelines: "You wanted equality? Well, then, deal with it!" The stronger the woman, the more she takes upon herself, and the more she should seek autonomy and independence, specifically in preparation for the coming hard times and troubles.

But if a woman feels the need, or the perfectly normal desire, to be by the side of a man who is deserving of her, to lean on his shoulder for support—a man who is capable of defending her and her children—then this man must possess the qualities which we very much need and value: trustworthiness, courage, honesty, frankness. Men, we need you! We need you to teach our children not to bow their heads but to fight, in order to create a future in which they will one day become free!

5 *Arnica montana*, https://en.wikipedia.org/wiki/Arnica

After all, if there is to be salvation, then it is to be found not somewhere far away, but in ourselves, in family life, in family harmony within a close circle of friends.

Claire Severac
Author of the following books:
Global conspiracy against health (Complot mondial contre la santé)

Food is the Best Medicine (Les aliments sont les meilleurs médicaments)

Enough! Our children are more important than the CAC 40[6] (La coupe est pleine : Nos enfants sont plus précieux que le CAC 40)

---

6 CAC 40 (*Cotation Assistée Continue*) is the most important French stock index, computed from the stock prices of the country's 40 largest companies—*Editor's note*.

To Margarita

Margarita

"She works hard for the money,
so hard for it honey.
She works hard for the money,
so you better treat her right."
–Donna Summer (1948-2012)

Margarita could have become an imperial marshal, if only she were born 130 years earlier and if she were a man. But she was born a woman, in 1904, into a working-class family in Torino, the capital of Piedmont, in the Kingdom of Italy.

Margarita was the eldest of six children. Everyone called her by the diminutive Rita. She received no education beyond primary, having been expelled from school after she slapped a teacher, who, the girl thought, had unfairly punished her younger sister Giovanna. And so, at the age of 12, Margarita started working at a factory. It was Venchi,[7] a chocolate and candy factory. There she worked at a conveyor belt, placing biscuits and chocolates in paper wrappers, then packing them in cardboard boxes and tins, just like in the famous scene from Charlie Chaplin's film *Modern Times*. Her salary was two lira a month.

In order to increase this pauper's wage she soon started offering her services to the director of the factory, a woman who was also the daughter the owner and founder. She took home her laundry and brought it back the next day clean and ironed. For this service, in addition to a small increase to her official salary, she obtained the right to take home candy waste. This

---

7 http://it.wikipedia.org/wiki/Venchi

allowed her to procure for her family a small amount of additional food.

At 17 years of age she married Pierino, a young soldier back from the trenches of World War I, who found a job as a railroad worker in Turin. Margarita managed so save enough money to open a small flower shop in a busy place—next to the entrance to Turin's public cemetery.

Margarita could barely read and write, but she could count well. She also knew how to treat her clients well, conscientiously inserting kind words, light flattery, and expressing her condolences with sincerity. This led the clients to buy a more expensive bouquet, a larger wreath... with flowers that hadn't yet wilted—which she had no qualms about taking back after the funeral was over, and selling them again at a discount to those of more humble means. Money is money, nothing was wasted, and everybody was happy!

In 1924 Margarita gave birth to her first daughter, Cesarina, who died from meningitis at 18 months. Then, in 1936, she gave birth to her second daughter, the little Rosanna, who died at 10 months from whooping cough. These two tragedies brought huge suffering to the young mother and to her husband. It is not the least bit surprising that from that moment on Margarita's husband developed serious addictions to alcohol and tobacco.

In the June of 1940 a new drama unfolded: war was declared against France and the United Kingdom. This unpopular war became a catastrophe for Italy. Pierino was mobilized, and promised that should he return alive, they will again try to have a child. He fulfilled his promise. In 1942 a little boy was born, whose life history will be subject of another book.

During the war the family left Turin and settled in a village, in order to avoid Anglo-American bombardments and, more importantly, to be closer to relatives who farmed. With their help, and also by doing a bit of trading on the black market, the family managed to eat reasonably well during this difficult time.

In 1945 Margarita resumed her job as a florist.

During Italy's post-war economic boom and the "Italian economic miracle" Margarita managed to buy an apartment and to send her only son to study at the prestigious Avogadro Technical Institute.[8] He became one of the first Italian engineers in the field of information technology. When he graduated from the institute, Margarita bought him a Fiat 500. She always spoke with pride of this social achievement, hers and her son's—but also with the suppressed rage of someone who had exacted revenge against the vicissitudes of fortune.

After the death of her husband in 1966 Margarita sold her flower shop and successfully invested the money in real estate. She was well provided for in her old age, but she always remained frugal, knowing that every penny is a penny, earned through sweat and toil. I remember how every Christmas and on each birthday she gave me a small gold coin. That is what, many years later, allowed me to become financially independent.

Margarita Zola was my grandmother. She died in 1993, having traversed the 20th century with all of its sorrows, tragedies and sufferings, individual and common. From her position at the very bottom of the social hierarchy in economically and

---

8 http://it.wikipedia.org/wiki/istituto_tecnico_industriale_statale_am edeo_ avogadro

11

socially backward Italy, she witnessed the birth of the modern state, economic growth and the establishment of individual freedoms, which allowed a woman of very humble origins to become independent and, relying only on herself, to fashion her life the way she wanted. She succeeded in doing so in spite of personal tragedies which are difficult for us to even imagine. Nobody could tell her how to behave, and nobody could compel her to follow orders.

In the old age home, where Margarita spent the last two years of her life, she terrorized the personnel and rewrote the schedules and the rules so that they suited her rather than the other way around! Even the tax inspectors couldn't get at her, but that's a different story, and also quite specifically Italian...

My grandmother was a survivor, a warrior, a woman who demanded universal obedience and earned universal respect. By all rights, she had earned her nickname of "general in chief," whispered by her neighbors and relatives behind her back. In my eyes, she symbolizes a certain life path of women of the last century. This path was often difficult, sometimes tragic and full of suffering, but also liberating and empowering.

I hope that on that long road she was able to find her happiness.

"There are two ways of spreading light: to be the candle or the mirror that reflects it."
–Edith Whorton, American writer (1862-1937)

"Nothing in life is to be feared, it is only to be understood. Now is the time to understand more, so that we may fear less."
–Marie Curie, Polish physicist (1867-1934)

Part I: The Century of Women

> "I myself have never been able to find out precisely what feminism is: I only know that people call me a feminist whenever I express sentiments that differentiate me from a doormat."
> –Rebecca West, English writer (1892-1983)

> "One is not born a woman, but becomes one."
> –Simone de Beauvoir, French feminist (1908-1986)

In just a few generations we have wandered far from nature in our habits and our way of life, which had previously flowed within a rhythm set by the seasons, defined by a multitude of everyday pressing problems and controlled by precise and strict social norms. This transformation, which became possible thanks to science, technology, economics and agribusiness, has fundamentally altered politics, culture[9] and all aspects of our daily life.

Modern medicine, electricity, cheap energy, railroads, cars, airlines, landline and mobile telephones, air conditioning, central heating, all sorts of household technology, video and other information technologies, even potable water on tap, have become the infrastructure and the technologies which, over the course of the last two centuries, have allowed Europeans to escape the need to survive through hard and uncertain daily toil.

The changes which transpired in the West have by now reached even the remotest corners of the world. Deep in agrarian China, in every village in India or the African continent, in the hard-to-reach places of the Amazon basin, everyone is opening themselves up—for better or for worse—to the paradigm of civilization in which individuality, culture, rights, education, leisure, means of self-fulfillment and professional opportunities are entirely different from what was traditional just a few years ago. These traditions were, we have to agree, sometimes feudal, cruel, full of coercion and constraints—again, for better or for worse.

If these developments, which took place in the course of history, brought freedom to innumerable people, then first and foremost they liberated women: fashion, progress in personal hygiene, contraception, modernized living arrangements, access to education, indoor plumbing, social and professional integration, diversification of social roles, rights and status... Billions among them found the collision between traditional, often centuries-old culture, and modernity, which was often synonymous with the loss of cultural identity, the

9 Florence Montreynaud, *Le XXe siècle des femmes*, éditions Nathan, 1988.

softening of social mores, sexual ones especially, quite painful. Often it gave rise to resistance and conflicts, sometimes violent ones.

In spite of all these conflicts, the irresistible march toward the emancipation of women gave them access to freedoms which were previously very rare and only available to a tiny elite.

Women (and men) evolve from monkeys[10]

If we look back into the remote, very remote, past, we will see that biological differences between men and women were the natural result of their specialized roles within the group.

If we go back as far as the Cromagnons, or even farther, as far as the various ancestors of the primates of the genus *Homo* —*ergaster* (the worker), *habilis* (the handy), *afarensis, australopithecus*—then we will see that these were all mammals that led a complex social life. Social life was always vitally important, because we never were at the top of the food chain. Without sharp claws, unable to run as fast as our natural predators (we served as food for lions, leopards and other large cats), relatively weak physically (we lack an exoskeleton and have a vulnerable, soft belly)... our ancestors couldn't have survived were it not for their social structure and their use of tools, which grew in sophistication because of the amazing development of our brains, which was in turn made possible by the vertical orientation of our bodies, which freed our hands, and by an increasingly varied and flexible diet.

---

10 And monkeys climbed down from the trees.

Moreover, nature imposed upon the human female (woman, that is) a 9-month pregnancy, a relatively difficult birth, a lengthy period of nursing and, finally, the need to care for offspring over several years, during which it cannot exist autonomously. Such constraints, which are necessary for the developments of a brain as large as ours, forced us into a communal existence, and into separation of labor. Essentially, during pregnancy and while nursing and caring for children a woman was naturally driven to specialize in caring for the home, bringing up the children and in handling associated tasks, such as gathering and preparing food, making clothing, helping other women in the group and to some extent—this was taken for granted—in defense and hunting.

The male of the species (man, that is) had a musculature, skin and skeleton better suited for physical contact and violence, and specialized in areas that required brute strength—hunting and defense of the group—tasks at which he excelled thanks to his physical strength and inventiveness. As paleontological evidence makes clear, such activities did not preclude men from participating in gathering food, making tools, creative self-expression, bringing up children and so on—tasks in which they engaged with the help of women, of course.

In addition, these tendencies toward specialization[11] were conditioned by two different social instincts, which are easy to observe even in our days: on the one hand, the "nurturing" instinct, directed toward society and the relationships within the group; on the other, the "declarative" instinct, which is directed more toward individuality.[12]

---

11 White D., Brudner L., Burton M. *Sexual Division of Labor*, 1977.

The "declarative" instinct is based, among other things, on our basic needs (competing for mates, the urge to occupy the dominant position in a certain social hierarchy—yesterday the best hunter, today whoever climbs higher in the social or economic ladder), while the "nurturing" instinct is directed mainly toward teaching, caring for and bringing up children, as well as cooperation and the search for the best possible protection.

Warning! This is not a question of absolute traits but merely tendencies. Men can perfectly well follow the "nurturing" instinct, and the women can perfectly well follow the "declarative" one.

In this way, the union between a man and a woman should be understood as the smallest productive unit within any society. This is first of all a functional structure for survival, and it has more advantages than inconveniences.

To this base structure, which is necessary for survival, are connected various other social structures which humankind has created over time. For a man, a woman is the giver of life, and is magic, as evidenced by the earliest sculptural renderings of women, but the moment a man realizes that he too plays a certain part in reproduction, his respect for the woman becomes weaker and more narcissistic, because now it is directed toward the mother of his children. Obviously, this is not some universal truth, since there are other modes of social and family functioning,[13] but this is the one that is found in the vast majority of cases throughout the world and throughout

12 See the works of Dr. C. George Boeree, professor of the University of Schippensburg, Pennsylvania, specialist in the history of psychology and personality theory.

history, and it exerts a definite influence on social structures which regulate the relationships between men and women.

The history of power

In certain ancient tribes and cultures we can observe very strongly egalitarian relations between men and women. For example, the women of the Nigerian culture Aka hunted and exercised control over the distribution of resources which they took part in procuring. In the 4th century BCE 40 percent of the land in Sparta belonged to women, who were more or less the equals of men. They had the right to divorce without loss of property, and throughout the Hellenistic period the wealthiest citizens of Sparta were women.

Gradually, more patriarchal cultures emerged. They limited the role of women and codified it in their laws, both civil and religious.

In the case of the Roman West, for example, only maternity was considered natural, while paternity was regarded as cultural and therefore regulated by the civil code. The institution of marriage inherited a cruel gender-based and cultural repression, making women the wards of men in an effort to guarantee the certainty of their paternity.[14]

This cultural approach persisted over many centuries. In Europe and in the countries of the Mediterranean it appeared due to Roman expansion, and then through the church. The

---

13 For example, the Moso ethnicity, peoples that commonly practice polygamy, etc.

14 *Mater semper certa est, pater est semper incertus, pateris est quem nuptiae demonstrant.* (Mother is always know for certain, father is not known for certain, father is determined by marriage.)

church, which was constructed on the basis of Greco-Roman philosophy, and using the existing infrastructure of the Roman Empire, which embraced Christianity as the official religion[15] in the 3rd century, permitted this culture to be maintained. Subsequently, due to European expansion after the Renaissance, this culture took root on the American continent.

In the Near East a similar phenomenon appeared in Islamic culture and its expansion along the southern shore of the Mediterranean, the Middle East and Central Asia. We also see the appearance of a more nuanced form of patriarchy in the cultures of China, India and other Asian countries.

In this way, the desire to control, prejudices, customs and, at times, superstitions were gradually codified in the laws, to eventually drastically limit the sphere of activity and the rights of women in the majority of societies. Specifically, they excluded:

- The right to physical inviolability and autonomy
- The right to own property
- The right to equal treatment before the law
- The right to work
- The right to receive an education
- The right of free self-expression
- The right to divorce
- The right to vote
- The right to hold public office
- The right to consciously terminate pregnancy
- The right to contraception
- The right to equal pay for equal work

15 The Christianization of the Roman Empire was made official by Constantine I in 312 AD.

21

Women in the 20th century

Many calls to soften the laws that restricted the rights of women in society were already being heard in the 19th century. However, it was only the start of the 20th century that became both a symbolic and a real watershed moment for women in the West. There is no doubt that 1914 was the point of departure for reforms that transformed the social, psychological, political and economic terrain.[16]

In reality, in 1914, with the start of World War I,[17] as a consequence of mass mobilization of male labor, many women, who until then had no income, started to work in weapons factories and, on a larger scale, in production and agriculture. Mechanization, as well as Taylorism and Fordism,[18] the motive forces of economic expansion, allowed women, in spite of their lack of qualifications, to get work which was previously considered exclusively male. The wages paid to women, which were significantly about two-thirds—lower than the wages paid to men, soon became a serious motivating factor for employers. In search of profitability, they actively supported

---

16 To form an impression about the progressive ideas of the 19th century, see the work of Pierre-Joseph Proudhon, *Pornocracy: Women in present time* (*La Pornocratie, ou les femmes dans les Temps modernes*), 1875.

17 This same process appeared in part in the United States during the War of Independence.

18 These are forms of organizing labor for maximizing profits within a single organization. They included a detailed analysis of methods and technologies of production (movement, rhythm, frequency), the implementation of the most effective forms of production (distribution of responsibilities), standardization of parts and units of assembly, as well as the development of effective and motivated means of compensation.

making permanent the role of women in the process of production. Moreover, in all the countries involved in this conflict, women's capacity to work was regarded as a decisive factor. The emerging propaganda narrative of the time tried to instill in the collective unconscious the idea that women can work alongside men in factories, in the fields, in hospitals, in administration, without the help of men, and for the first time make their contribution to the defense and the survival of the group, represented as the Nation.

In just a few years we went from a feminine realm that was previously restricted to domestic activities, in line with the philosophic traditions of Plato and Aristotle,[19] to the realm of large factories of the second industrial revolution. This new vision for the role of women in society fundamentally overturned their perspectives and their demands for rights and social status on the labor market.

With the mass involvement of women in the labor market (during the second industrial revolution they comprised approximately a third of the economically active population), promising them some measure of economic independence, the family unit started a slow transformation. It was not too rare for the new women-workers to encounter violent opposition of certain parts of society, which were strongly attached to the traditional distribution of gender roles, and which tried to

---

19 A synthesis of *The Myth of the Cave*, *The Republic* and *The Laws* of Plato and many works by Aristotle is possible and allowable. According to the opinions of these philosophers, the main activity of women consisted of preserving the property created by men. The work of women had no value for them, since "the science of earning a living is not equivalent to the art of household work."

limit women to domestic labor and the rearing of children.

From this economic boom, which was initially nurtured through the great efforts demanded by World War I, new demands appeared and spread over time; for example, giving women the right to vote and other political rights.

Previously to this period, universal suffrage (*suffrage universel*, a term coined by Diderot in 1765) did not presuppose the participation of all women, and, in some countries, even of working-class men, peasants and persons of color. However, the concept was advanced based on the principle of free expression of people's will, of the entire citizenry as the embodiment of the sovereignty of the nation. Under a regime that claimed to be democratic such an anomaly could no longer exist.

The first country to guarantee women the right to vote was New Zealand in 1893. Australia followed its example in 1902, Finland in 1906, Norway in 1913, Denmark and Iceland in 1915. After the end of World War I the entire Western world gradually gave women the right to vote:

The Netherlands: 1917
Austria, Canada, Georgia, Czechoslovakia, Poland, Sweden, Russia: 1918
Germany, Luxembourg: 1919
United States: 1920
Great Britain: 1918
Turkey: 1930
Spain: 1931
Thailand, Brazil: 1932
France: 1944

Belgium, Italy, Rumania, Japan, Yugoslavia: 1946
Israel: 1948
Greece, India, Lebanon: 1952
Tunisia: 1957
Iran, Afghanistan: 1963
Switzerland: 1971
Saudi Arabia: 2011

If the industrial revolutions and World War I signaled the fraying of certain barriers for women,[20] then it was World War II, when millions of women were recruited into both industry and the military, that allowed them to fortify their breach into the labor market, and to demand numerous new rights.

During World War II just the British armed services drafted 460,000 women. The majority of them were assigned to air de-fense forces that repelled attacks by German bombers and V-1 flying bombs, but they also worked in logistics and transporta-tion. In addition, hundreds of thousands of British women were recruited in industry and manufacturing: munitions and ordnance, shipbuilding, assembly line work in aircraft and au-tomobile manufacturing, armaments and so forth.

Outside of manufacturing and the professions directly as-sociated with the war effort, women became indispensable in other existentially important fields, such as firewood harvest-ing and, most importantly, in agriculture. Over just a few years, having replaced men who were sent to the front, British women, of few means and for the most part continuing to care

20 In 1928 the book *The Wonderful Wizard of Oz* by Frank Baum was banned in all the libraries in Chicago, US, because it showed women "in positions of leadership."

for their children, managed to triple the agricultural production of the United Kingdom.

In the Soviet Union more than 820,000 women volunteered in the army as doctors, nurses, radio operators, artillery spotters, snipers,[21] fighter pilots and officers. Praises for their achievements in the Great Patriotic War are sung to this day.

In Germany representatives of the "weaker sex" willingly joined the "Union of German Maidens,"[22] or in the "Werwolf"[23] guerrilla groups. They cut off retreat and resupply paths, carried out night raids, blew up military, commercial and civil installations, and killed those who wanted to surrender or collaborate with the enemy.

In France, after the defeat of 1940 and the appointment to power of marshal Philippe Pétain, French women went through a counter-reform of the role of women in society, mainly with an eye toward inducing population growth, which

---

21 Of the 2,000 Soviet women who became snipers during 1941-1945, the best-known is Lyudmila Pavlichenko, Ukrainian by birth. She used the Tokarev SVD-40 with an ×3.5 optical sight to eliminate 309 enemy soldiers.

22 *Bund Deutscher Mädel*—a movement of girls between 14 and 18, which was essentially the female wing of the youth movement Hitlerjugend. The union organized summer camps, trips out to nature, all in the Nazi spirit, in order to inculcate in the girls the principles of the Third Reich concerning the status of women in family and society.

23 *Werwolf* was a type of Nazi fighting force organized for partisan warfare, spreading terror and creation of underground networks. The German military command created it at the end of World War II in order to oppose the Allies behind the front, specifically on the eastern front. (See the practical guide *Werwolf-Winke für Jagdeinheinten*, published in January of 1945.

again defined women as housewives. One of the strategies pursued by the Vichy government was the establishment in 1941 of a "Mother's Day,"[24] aimed at boosting population growth and preserving old ways of thinking and a culture in which the woman, being the main pillar of the family, can only devote herself to the joys of motherhood and romantic feelings, but can play no part in production or defense. In a speech he delivered on that occasion, marshal Pétain declared: "Mothers of our France! Your task is the most difficult, but also the most beautiful. You, even before the government, provide upbringing. Only you know how to inculcate the desire to work, discipline, modesty, respect, which make people saintly and nations strong."[25]

We find a similar mindset in the words of another historical figure, in this case an Iranian: ayatollah[26] Khomeini: "A woman is the embodiment of a man's most sacred wishes. She is the nurturer of deserving women and men... Without her founding role, nations would fall into decadence. Women bring up children and, consequently, they are the first who can convey the good word to future generations."[27]

But in most Western countries, in spite of much popular opposition, a significant number of women entered resistance

24 A day for "mothers of many children" existed since 1920. The French government made an official "Mother's Day" in 1929 in order to facilitate conducting a policy aimed at boosting population growth. See http://www.marechal-petain/avesetopinions/fetedemeres.htm.

25 Speech of May 25, 1941.

26 *Ayatollah* is a Shiite religious title given to one knowledgeable in the theory and practice of Islam who has the right to issue a *fatwah*—a decision based on Sharia law—*Editor's note*.

27 Imam Ruhollah Khomeini, *Sahifey-ye Imam*, Vol. 7 p. 341, 179

movements, and a minority of them even took part in combat operations. While numerous women joined partisan movements in Italy, Greece, Yugoslavia, Poland and the Soviet Union, where they struck fear into the hearts of the enemy, women who participated in the French Resistance were often shunted into secondary roles. But some of them, such as Lucie Aubrac, Hélène Vianney and Marie-Madeleine Fourcade,[28] played leading roles in the war conducted by the "shadow army."

After the end of World War II most European countries experienced not just an economic but a demographic boom. It was quite common for a woman to give birth to three, four or even five children, while continuing to work in a factory. This was the famous "baby boom"—the peak of population growth, which gave rise to a quite populous generation which has come to be called "baby boomers."

Women had to learn to maintain a new, precarious balance: on the one hand, they exalted in their new, liberating economic and political power, symbolized by figures such as Rosie the Riveter and their acts of technical prowess such as the first woman in space;[29] on the other, their family realm was still burdened by Platonic sociocultural baggage, which demanded of women that they remain the keepers of the family hearth while continuing to work, often having the very low status of "the working class of the working class."[30]

---

28 She was the leader of one of the largest cells of the Resistance, was captured twice, but escaped each time.
29 Citizen of the USSR Valentina Tereshkova ascended to Earth orbit on June 16, 1963.

During this same period American industry, which in 1950 comprised more than 50 percent of the entire world's industrial activity, switched from manufacturing armaments to making consumer goods, with the aim of preserving profits.

It manufactured millions of vacuum cleaners, ovens equipped with timers and clocks, refrigerators so large they had to be restocked just once a week, millions of washing machines which reduced heavy domestic labor from two days to a few hours a week, mixers, pots with anti-stick coatings, bread machines, kitchen combines and automatic coffee-makers, allowing women to save a great deal of time. Without the free time made possible by these new mechanisms, which during that period were high-quality and durable, "women's liberation" would have only been achievable for those few who could have delegated this work to others: housekeepers, nannies, wet-nurses and so on. The revolution in the sphere of household technology paved the way for the appearance of our consumer society.

This saved time gave women the opportunity to demonstrate that they are capable of much more than traditional society believed. It made it possible for them to pass into law or win support for demands which went much further than the right to vote or the right to own property. The battle over the gender role of women was about to start, over their role as heads of family and, finally, over absolute equal rights.

Starting in the 1960s, new laws went into effect concerning domestic violence, divorce, defense of children, adoption and

---

30 We took this definition from the brochure People's Union by Flora Tristan, published in 1843. See Tristan, F. L'Union ouvrière.

contraception (such as the Neuwirth law in France[31]). This second wave of "liberation" was heavily influenced by the public declarations of certain women against traditional views of the woman's domestic role. Many bras were set on fire, and lots of men and women experimented with drugs and free love. This led to a rethinking of all that was previously considered to be "normal" in music, mores, world views, freedom... for better or for worse.

Women's liberation... but liberation from what?

Historically, those who accelerated the process of women's liberation were often rich and influential men[32] whose intentions were most often based on a pressing economic calculus rather than any altruistic desire dripping with kindness and empathy for the social, political or economic conditions of the

---

31 The Neuwirth law was adopted by the National Assembly on December 19, 1967, authorizing the use of contraceptives, notably, oral contraceptives. Named after Lucien Neuwirth, the Gaullist deputy who proposed it, this law overturned the law of July 31, 1920, which had banned all contraception.

32 For example, Edward Bernays, the creator of modern propaganda (whose book *Propaganda*, 1928, became the foundation of contemporary marketing) promoted women's right to smoke when he worked for the American Tobacco Company. Another example is the Rockefeller Fund which fought for women's emancipation. One of the heirs of this famous family, Nicholas Rockefeller, in 2000 told the film director Aaron Russo: "We stand at the headwaters of women's liberation. We had newspapers, television, the Rockefeller Fund... We did this for two reasons: so that it wasn't possible to just tax half the population, and so that children could start school sooner. In this way, it was easier for us to propagandize them, and we could break family ties."

"second sex."

In parallel, many feminist movements attempted to distinguish women from men and to turn them into a special, separate social category. If there exists a diversity of significant differences between people (rich and poor, skinny and fat, tall and short, happy and sad, smart and...) then does there exist a feminine nature, common to all women?

One must be very careful when analyzing women's liberation movements and their fight for their rights, because it is very easy to fall into the trap of systematically opposing the two sexes, if not start a war of women against men.

In essence, if nature imposes on women the necessity of giving birth, then this cannot be considered a form of social oppression nefariously contrived by men. Moreover, it is not possible to declare that, in principle, all women at all times have been oppressed, because history counts among them priestesses, queens, courtesans, free-thinkers, writers, grifters, warriors, scientists, explorers...[33]

Finally, let us not lose track of the real position of contemporary women, who often have to combine their work as a mother with the work of a shop clerk, administrator, assistant, social worker... Surviving with difficulty on just one income, women find themselves in danger of unemployment in the unfolding crisis, and are subject to social pressure, of varying intensity, depending on the local culture, which demands of her that she remain seductive, feminine and sexy.

---

33 We have in mind: Eleanor of Aquitaine, Catherine Medici, Isabella of Castille, Catherine the Great, Boadicea, Janne D'Arc, the salon of Mme. de Stahl, the laboratory of Hypatia of Alexandria or, closer to our time, of Marie Curie, as well as the pilot Amelia Earhart.

In reality, the fight for women's liberation could be regarded as a component of the fight for the liberation of men, so that together we can free all of us from alienating conditions of life.

But it is undeniable that the situation of women is too often very difficult.

According to the statistics, 72 percent of 50-year-old women work, and 90 percent of women at some point in their lives are forced to independently secure their financial independence.[34] In 2008, in the US, the average weekly salary of women who worked full-time was 20 percent lower than that of their male counterparts. In France, this figure stood at 18 percent.[35] Female employees are often the only wage-earners within their families, while the majority of them remain trapped in low-paying positions. More than two-thirds of them are employed part-time, and thus have less job security and are deprived of most benefits provided by employers.

When it comes to women who devote themselves body and soul to prestigious and better-compensated careers, by the time they are 40 they often end up lonely and childless, realizing that they sacrificed the best years of their lives enriching some financial organization that is usually led by men!

Finally, women who belong to the highest social class, by inheritance or by marriage, belong to a social category that traditionally exploits women-workers. History attests to the curious fact that the majority of feminists emerged from just this milieu, and while they strove to liberate their "sisters"

---

34 Data from Institut National de la Statistique et des Études Economiques (INSEE), France—*Editor's note.*
35 INSEE.

from exploitation by "men," they themselves, they showed not a moment's hesitation in delegating subordinate tasks, such as doing household labor or bringing up children, to their maids and nannies!

To the above we must add that quite frequently the role of women in giving birth and bring up children receives insufficient credit from either the masculine conception of the world or the feminist one.

In consequence, women, who were traditionally co-owners and co-directors of a small enterprise—to wit, the family, in which they performed prestigious and beneficial work (specifically, loving care and bringing-up of children), but which was not recognized as such—in our days most of them have ended up working as low-level servants or hired labor, with low pay, in an enterprise that does not belong to them.

Perhaps the main enemy of women is not man but the phe-nomenon which the French writer Vivianne Forrester called "the economic horror."[36]

Consumerism is increasingly feminized

On television, on billboards, in the press, on the internet, everywhere... consumer society weaponizes women in order to sell. This is very simple to do: images of women are used in ad-vertising, their bodies systematically displayed on product packaging, to entice men to buy. Women are also targeted, be-cause their desire to seduce and their fear of their younger, more beautiful rivals are also exploited, in order to entice them to consume everything that the fashion magazines offer:

---

36 Forrester, V. L'Horreur économique, 1996.

cosmetics, fashionable clothing and all the associated products.

As an example,[37] let's take one of the fashion magazines, *Elle*, published by Hachette Filipacchi Médias, which belongs to the media group Lagardère.[38] This magazine one of the best-known in the so-called "women's" press. Founded in 1945, it is currently being printed in about 500,000 copies a month, of which 180,000 are sent to subscribers.

A copy chosen at random was No. 3519 from June 7, 2013. Of its 178 pages, 72 pages, or 40 percent, are occupied by advertising, and 30 pages, or 16 percent, by fashion and style.

As far as the contents, here they are:

• Page 18—latest news: Glamor in Venice; Istanbul: toward a Turkish spring? Rolland-Garros—game set and smack! Souhir Ben Amra: an actress in the Tunisian revolution; Laure Heriard Dubreuil, the proud shopper: is she the most powerful woman in fashion? Michael Douglas: a dangerous tumor. *Chime for Change:*[39] women in concert.

• Page 37—Culture: Laura Mvula—UFO singer; Theater: married at any price, how to handle coming out;[40] Art criticism: Exposition of buttocks painted by Reubens; Show of the week: Versailles is fashionable; Television: shows "Odysseus," "The

---

37 A similar analysis was attempted by the sociologist Alain Soral. See Soral, A., *Vers la féminisation? Démontage d'un complot anti-démocratique*, 2007.

38 Its sales volume in 2012 was 7.37 billion Euro.

39 A social organization founded by Gucci for helping women in third-world countries—*Editor's note*.

40 Coming out as gay.

Vikings" and "The Queen of Shopping."

a bicycling holiday. Tests: five lessons of make-up. Psychology: mother-daughter, how to use. Advice: a 100 percent antitoxic life. Fitness: coaching gym express. Personal life: one day with May Lan.

What conclusion can we draw from reading such a magazine? That freedom has been reduced to the imperative of seduction, and the female readers are persistently advised to spend money on fashionable products, cosmetics, products for losing weight and preserving beauty. That what little information remains has been boiled down to tourism and chitchat, all the while deploring the fact that so many women all around the world are as yet unable to join in with the mass consumption. That feminism allows us to gush over the success of this or that artist, singer or actor. That even important subjects, such as breast cancer, can only be exemplified by celebrities. That culture has been reduced to fashion, cosmetics, interior decoration and society gossip. That the image of a woman, with the measurements of a mannequin—that is, borderline anorexic, very young, beautiful, "exotic"—has nothing to do with reality. Finally, that science is absent except as exemplified by astrology and numerology.

This reduction of thought and information to pop psychology is summed up by the title the horoscope section: "Personal realm, intuition, emotion."

Meanwhile, what's on television is even worse.[41]

I don't mean to stigmatize or to ridicule, but simply to point out that, in a world where the only economic goal is turning a quick profit, absolutely everything, in the most natural way, forces women—and men, for we could expand at length about the fantastic level of interest of many men in sports, cars, and illustrated men's magazines devoted to them, to say nothing of the new magazines for metrosexuals and gays—to turn into beings whose freedom is reduced to desire, and desire—to the act of consumption.

Everything is being done for the sake of just that.

This is too bad, but it is a logic of which women must become conscious, and this realization should prompt them to learn something new, because otherwise a century of struggle for emancipation and freedom will only lead to changing the type of alienation to a more pretentious and dangerous dependency.

The 21st Century of Women?

Over the past hundred years, the gains in rights, comforts and liberties won by all the men and women throughout the world have been undeniable and spectacular. They have contributed more or less directly to women becoming, by the beginning of the 21st century, the equals of men, at least in

41 See Desmurgets M. *TV Lobotomie—La vérité scientifique sur les effets de la télévision* (*TV Lobotomy: The Scientific Truth about the Effects of Television*), 2012.

37

terms of rights.

Nevertheless, it is important to always remember that it is not possible to dissociate the process of women's liberation from the ever-increasing use of fossil fuel energy, from the development of modern medicine, mechanization, standardization, technological revolution, dynamic development of infrastructure and systems of supply and distribution, and intensive agribusiness. Everything is interconnected...

We have entered into an era of endless growth, system-wide optimization and ever-increasing demands, even if they do grave harm to quality and integrity, even if they cannot give meaning to the lives of the teeming masses of humanity...

But endless growth is impossible in a world whose resources are by definition limited. Although the 20th century allowed women to achieve significant progress, our contemporary 21st century is as fragile as it is complex.

2. The Modern World

"If a woman is sufficiently ambitious,
determined and gifted—there is practically nothing she can't do."
—Helen Lorenson, American writer and
feminist (1908-1982)

"The trouble with the rat race is that
even if you win, you're still a rat."
—Lily Tomlin, American actress

Our modern world is fantastic.

When we are thirsty, the water tap immediately provides us
with drinking water. When we want to eat, we can go and shop
at a supermarket, and there find just about any product during
just about any time of year and at almost any hour. If we feel
cold, we can turn up the thermostat. If we want to travel
somewhere, then there is the bicycle, the car, the metro, a
train or a plane to deliver us to our destination of our choice. If

we get sick, the hospitals and specially trained medical teams will take care of us... and if we feel tired, angry or sad, then a good hot shower, a DVD, a Nutella sandwich and a soft bed await us.

Electricity, central heating, indoor plumbing, cheap gasoline, modern medications, pharmacies, supermarkets, shopping malls, restaurants, museums, movie theaters, public transportation, the internet, airports... Never in our history have we achieved a period so plentiful and rich in comforts.

All of us—men, women and children—have benefited greatly from these comforts, which become ever more integral to our way of life, and the construction of this modernity has played an essential role in the process of women's emancipation and flowering. This quest for comfort, at the moment, seems to run in a single direction—toward "more and more," with any backtracking both undesirable and impossible.

Nobody would want—and especially not women, who have just recently gained their relative freedom—to return to primitive and archaic lifestyles, mindsets or technologies. Nobody would want that, especially not us—the superconsumers of disposable shavers, cocoa-scented bubble baths, iPhones and pain killers!

We regard as utterly obsolete such things as bloodletting, the Bubonic plague, the fires of the Inquisition,[42] the swords of the Islamic guards,[43] wooden clogs, 40-year life expectancy and

---

42 The Inquisition burned at the stake between 3,000 and 5,000 people.
43 In this context the modern criminal code of Saudi Arabia is particularly interesting. It is based on the harsh Islamic Sharia law. Women who are caught committing adultery can be stoned to death, albeit this not being applied often. See Mackey, S., The Saudis: *Inside the Desert*

manual labor—all of these conjure up images that are repugnant to most of us. No doubt, the tiny minority of individuals who think the contrary and might dream of returning to an inadequately understood "tradition" find it difficult to integrate into our society, which is developing far too quickly for them. But the majority of us realize that we have been born during quite a convenient epoch, especially if we compare it with the middle ages in northern European countries.[44]

This dynamic of "progress" is very old. Essentially, the optimization of our world, and of our everyday life is one of the most important elements among the evolutionary principles responsible for the development of our brain. This development programmed our species in such a way that we continuously strive to master and improve our environment, to produce new tools, to think up new discoveries and inventions, and to widen the boundaries of our of possibilities, both physical and intellectual.

Some 12,000 years ago the development of agriculture allowed humans to settle down. Later, the ever more rapid migration of the world's population into cities, especially in the 19th and the 20th centuries, transformed our way of life. All along, the search for ever more optimized and ever-greater levels of comfort has only been speeding up, across the entire world.

Kingdom.

44 This is more of a wink in the direction of scenes from films such as *Pulp Fiction* and *The Visitors*, and less of a certainty about the Middle Ages in general, which were quite civilized and quite prosperous in certain places (Florence, Baghdad, Samarkand, Hangzhou, Cuzco).

But this pursuit of exponentially greater comfort came at a price.

In addition to anxiety and depression, which first started to afflict the West and then became widespread and increasingly noticeable elsewhere; in addition to migration, the nomadic lifestyle embraced by many, and the globalization of culture; in addition to constantly worsening ecological problems, depletion of resources such as fresh water and crude oil; in addition to the effects of globalization and relocation of production on labor markets, wages and salaries; in addition to the appearance of new chronic diseases brought on by the consumption of products of agribusiness and the ubiquitous medical and pharmaceutical industries, which are all very much interested in reaping the highest profits in the shortest amount of time... in addition to all that we have listed here, there is an additional price to be paid, and it is equivalent to the additional risk.

The risk associated with complexity

Complexity is inherent in our contemporary world, and in our unquenchable thirst for more speed, productivity, growth and cheap resources, and it is before our eyes every day.

It is in our infrastructure and distribution systems, such as the billions of miles of pipes, wires and cables in our cities and under them. It is in the highways, bridges, railroads, ports and airports, in all the buildings equipped with elevators, air conditioning systems, household electronics... It is in the enterprises, offices, centers of commerce, factories, hospitals, schools, homes for the elderly... and, of course, the billions of cars, busses, trucks, intersections, traffic lights, ships, planes and satellites.

It is also in the global trading networks which allow hyper-markets to be filled with the food we eat. In order for these networks to continue functioning, there has to exist intensive agriculture, with reservoirs and irrigation pumps, fertilizers and pesticides, tractors and combines steered by satellite, with grain elevators and logistics centers. All of this is financed and controlled by a financial system that depends on stock values and commodity markets, and more and more of it works in a real-time regime using cloud-based internet services, and is ever more insulated from physical reality.

And all of this complexity has to function continuously, 24 hours a day, every day.

We are completely dependent on it.

Of course, our contemporary world is a fantastic machine that can save the life of a sick child or free a woman from hav-ing to depend on a man. But... it is a very fragile mechanism, specifically because of its complexity. The reality is that the modern world is a boundless tangle of a multitude of complex systems tied into a single network. A sudden break in any part of this system can cause instability, which can quickly spread and endanger the stability of the whole. And, in consequence, it can endanger our lives.

Among these unfathomable complexities—of which there are many—which contribute either directly or indirectly to the fragility of our world, there are some that represent a more decisive factor than others...

"Just in Time"

The concept of "just in time" came to us from Japan and was propagandized by the car company Toyota. It offers a particularly compelling illustration of the complexity of our world.

"Just in time" is a management system focused primarily on minimizing inventory. The goal is to deliver supplies only when there arises a need for them—when the order comes in—thus eliminating the unnecessary, if not to say wasteful, expenditures on warehousing them, controlling inventory, and disposing of out-of-date inventory of obsolete or expired products. Thanks to "smart" management techniques, it is also possible to save on the transportation costs of moving products to distribution centers, which also operate on "just in time" principles in supplying the end users.

This system, which was first introduced in the 1960s and 1970s, was considerably expanded and perfected in the 1990s and 2000s thanks, notably, to information technology, which now makes possible real-time control over the entire supply chain of almost all products, including fuel, food, medications, cars, commercial equipment, spare parts, consumer goods and so on, starting with the raw materials used in their manufacture and assembly and ending with their transportation, storage, wholesale and retail distribution... until they finally end up in your shopping cart, exactly when you need them—not a moment too early, not a moment too late.

In time this system came to monitor and predict consumer behavior. For the sake of homogeneity and profitability, the modern economic system did everything possible to influence us and, in the end, to make us adapt to it. A particularly direct and dramatic consequence of the "just in time" system is that we have stopped stockpiling supplies at home, since we can buy anything we need whenever the need arises. Small self-service shops, hypermarkets and internet-based vendors are always open for us. They offer everything we need and more, practically all the time. As a result all of us maintain a "zero supply cushion."

For example, large shopping centers and hypermarkets maintain inventory for just a few days. In order for their shelves to be stocked with the necessary minimum of goods, they must be constantly and regularly resupplied. The same is true for hospitals, clinics and pharmacies. They only maintain a two or three-day reserve of medications and medical supplies, without which the health care system would stop functioning.

At the level of the family, we who have become accustomed to this plenty of everything at all times, can cook no more than two or three meals from the supplies in our kitchens and pantries... It is very interesting to compare such habits with those of our grandmothers and grandfathers, for whom it was unthinkable to live without a stockpile of basic foodstuffs saved for the "rainy day." Based on their life experience, they could be quite sure that the "rainy day" would indeed come!

Specialization

Since, for lack of skill and time, we can't do everything and do it well, we always aim to do things that provide the highest reward. Thus we concentrate in areas in which we are the most talented, which are the least costly, and where we are the most productive. This is what is generally meant by "effectiveness." Effectiveness leads to profits. And effectiveness requires us to specialize.

Obviously, a plumber will achieve higher effectiveness if he concentrates exclusively on plumbing. Similarly, a public relations director of a large media group will not waste his time (unless the subject interests him as a hobby) on learning toilet installation and pipefitting. The same logic that applies to the trades applies to entire businesses and entire nations. This is by no means a new thought, and has been theorized by such thinkers as Plato, Adam Smith, David Ricardo, Karl Marx, Ludwig von Mises, Friedrich von Hayek and many others.

A similar tendency has always existed to one extent or another, but now it is a matter of absolute necessity as a matter of survival of any group. In the modern world, this notion of effectiveness, combined with globalization, growth and the principle of "just in time" has driven specialization to a high level of perfection, both in the area of skills and know-how and in the locations where they are deployed, resulting in a large boost in productivity and in higher profits.

However, this explosion in excessively narrow specialization within our modern societies can also result in severe imbalances:

- Today, in the majority of Western countries, just two percent of the population work in the primary productive sector; that is, making foodstuffs (through agriculture, fishing, etc.). This means that just two percent of the population feeds the remaining 98.

46

- Today, the farmers of North America receive more sub-sidies from the government for growing biofuels (specifically, ethanol) than for growing food.
- The majority of industrial centers that produce consumer goods, spare parts, equipment and pharmaceuticals are located in areas where production costs are extremely low.
- The vast majority of skills and specialized know-how, which were previously available relatively close to us, are now located very far away.

At this point, it is essential for us to realize that the majority of our products, medicines, machines, consumer products, as well as specialized skills now depend as never before on the correct, well-tuned functioning of transportation and communication networks.

The functioning of public administration depends on the collection of taxes and fees, which the government levies on citizens and businesses; citizens depend on their positions within organizations, thanks to which they receive money with which to pay taxes, as well as to buy food, consumer goods, pay for a place to live, pay the bills and so on. Businesses that employ them depend on their customers to buy their products and services. The infrastructure depends on all of this combined activity for its stability, as well as for the resources to develop, maintain and improve it.

Each part of society, and of the economic system, depends on the whole—whether directly or indirectly—for its proper functioning. This is what we are calling "interdependence."

Everything is interconnected. Because of this, any shock, any problem that arises in any one link of this very complex chain can have serious consequences for the system as a whole. The interconnections used to be at the scale of a country; but now, more than ever, everything is interconnected on a global scale. Events in China can affect Switzerland, and events in the Persian Gulf can raise the cost of fuel for your car. The reality of "the butterfly effect"[45] has never been more obvious:

- During the 2011 tsunami in northern Japan, the closing of local factories resulted in the shutdown of many assembly lines around the world, specifically automotive assembly plants in Europe, due to a shortage of electronic components.

- The cloud of ash thrown up by the Icelandic volcano Eyjafjallajökull, which temporarily shut down the airspace over Europe in 2010, all by itself threatened to cause certain hospitals to run out of pharmaceuticals that are manufactured on the opposite side of the Atlantic and delivered daily by air.

- In 2009 a snowstorm in northeastern United States completely disrupted down the delivery system for food and consumer goods, causing hardship for millions of people.

---

45 "The butterfly effect" is a metaphor for the basic phenomenon of a system whose behavior is greatly affected by an infinitesimally small difference in initial conditions, which is addressed by chaos theory. An event as insignificant as a butterfly fluttering its wings can in due course have serious consequences, such as affecting the course of a hurricane.

- In 2005 hurricane Katrina forced the shutdown of nine oil refineries in Louisiana and six in Mississippi, causing domestic refining capacity within the United States to fall by 20 percent and causing many gas stations to run out of gas.

Based on the example of the inhabitants of New Orleans, who tried to flee the city only to be trapped in gigantic traffic jams, or climbed the roofs of their houses in desperation, or sought shelter in the improvised "ark" of the Superdome, we can assess the vulnerability of our modern life, and the interdependence of the systems that support it.

Drought and forest fires in 2010 and 2011 in Russia caused a poor grain harvest and led to a ban on grain exports, causing grain prices to triple. This, in turn, could have led to starvation in certain countries in Africa.

Our modern world is at once all of this: a highly effective system full of possibilities, whether for its own technological development or for revolutionizing our social conditions (improved literacy, decreased infant mortality, access to education for women, tolerance of sexual and religious minorities...) but also full of of precariousness and vulnerability, often camouflaged by the vast intricacies of its technological potential.

At the start of the 21st century, lulled by the soothing comforts of our technologies, the question we should ask ourselves is the following: Have we not become as patients in a coma, hooked up to a more and more complex, fragile life support mechanism, and completely dependent on it?

And can it be that it is the women, in confronting a succession of crises, with their devastating, if not catastrophic, consequences, and especially in light of their achievements of the past hundred years, who stand to lose more than others?

3. Crisis

"Between two evils, I always pick the
one I never tried before."
—May West, American actress (1893-
1980)

"A woman is like a tea bag; you never
know how strong it is until it's in hot
water."
—Eleanor Roosevelt, American activist,
First Lady of the US (1884-1962)

"In life, nothing is to be feared, all is to
be understood."
—Marie Curie, Polish physicist (1867-
1934)

It is very difficult for a contemporary Westerner to understand, not at just an intellectual level, the reality of a world
without electricity, central heating, telephone networks, running water, sewer system, access to modern medicine, phar-

macies, security services, supermarkets full of products, cash machines...

All of these miracles of progress, all of these useful support systems designed to make our lives more convenient and easier have become synonymous with stable daily life.

Every day we take a hot shower, dress, take out the garbage, make coffee, charge our cell phone, watch news programs, ride the subway or a train, or drive a car, deposit money in a bank,[46] then withdraw it again from a cash machine, pay taxes, pay bills, cook food, check email... We consider all of this natural, habitual. In the final analysis, it represents a certain kind of homeostasis.[47]

Of course, this homeostatic scheme, this familiar normality, can fall apart, bringing on a crisis.

But what is a crisis? This word can signify multiple things: crisis in family relationships, teenage crisis, economic crisis, nervous breakdown, real estate crisis, unemployment crisis.

The word "crisis" is often thrown around needlessly. Nevertheless, it is possible to define it as a situation in which all that we are used to, all that soothes us and calms us, all that directly or indirectly relates to our homeostasis suddenly disap-

---

46 Since salaries, wages and benefits are now routinely deposited directly in our bank accounts, the banking system has come to play a central role in our lives.

47 Homeostasis (from the Greek ὅμοιος—like, and στάσις—stationary) is a term first introduced by Claude Bernard, and indicates the ability of a certain system (closed or open) to preserve dynamic equilibrium in spite of external disruptions. According to Walter Bradford Cannon, "homeostasis is a dynamic equilibrium that allows us to stay alive." It maintains the physiochemical parameters of an organism, such as the level of blood sugar, temperature, etc.

pears.

For example, a crisis may be brought on by a fire, a car accident, by civil unrest (as in the French suburbs in 2005), a natural catastrophe (as with the 2011 tsunami in Japan or the 1999 hurricane in Western Europe), or some form of violence, or an industrial or nuclear accident (such as the 2001 explosion at the AZF factory in Toulouse[48] or the 1986 nuclear catastrophe in Chernobyl), loss of employment, interruptions in the supply of water or electricity, a terrorist attack (as happened on rue de Rennes in Paris in 1986 or on September 11, 2011 in the United States) or an economic collapse (as in the former Soviet Union, Argentina, or more recently in Greece, Spain, Italy, soon to spread to France, Belgium, Germany...).

All of these events, all of these situations, all so different, as well as others, are quite likely, force us to face disequilibrium, and to wage battle against it as best we can.

Personal crisis

A personal crisis can erupt at any moment, at the scale of the individual or the family, and does so every day for millions of people around the world. It can be brought on by loss of employment, divorce, temporary or chronic depression, alcoholic dependency of a family member or a serious illness. It can also occur because of an auto accident, a flood, a fire that destroys the home, or a fall from a ladder. All of these can force us to deviate from our habits for a considerable period of time... But

48 This was an explosion at a chemical factory, as a result of which 30 people died and several thousand were harmed. The subsequent investigations went on for eight years. Among various versions of the cause were the improper storage of explosives and an act of terror.

that is life!

Here are some statistics for 2012 published by INSEE (France's national institute for statistics and economic research), France's ministry of internal affairs and the fire service:

- 317,900 fires, or a fire every two minutes
- 284,600 transportation-related accidents, or an accident every two minutes
- 3,082,400 cases where victims had to be assisted
- 2.9 million people, or ten percent of the economically active population, who are unemployed, and 3.7 million, or 13.5 percent, who would like to work but can't find a job (in the 4th quarter of 2012).
- Every day there are registered 363 divorces, or 132,594 a year (compared to 44,738 in 1972).
- Women file for divorce in 75 percent of cases.
- 44.7 percent of civil marriages fail. For comparison, in Sweden the level is 55 percent, 50 in Canada, 43 in the United Kingdom, 41.8 in Germany, 41 in the United States, 40.3 in Switzerland, 30.7 in Italy, 27 in Japan, 26 in Israel and 17 in Singapore.
- In 83 percent of cases the children remain with the mother.
- 1.6 million children thus live in newly formed families.
- Every year 1 percent of men and 3 percent of women fall into a nervous depression. The total number of cases of depression for the population as a whole is probably between 2-3 percent for men and 5-10 percent for women. In 2008 at least every fifth French

woman (21.4 percent) took psychoactive medication during the previous 12 months.[49] The probability of developing depression during one's entire life has risen to 10 percent for men and 20 percent for women.

Crisis due to criminality

Although the overall level of crime in the so-called "developed" countries is falling,[50] unfortunately violent crime and vandalism continue to exist, and in many cases to increase significantly. Whether frequent or not, theft, burglary, attacks, rapes and infliction of bodily harm—especially against women, who are often targeted—give rise to serious traumas and crises which are difficult for the victims to cope with.

According to the statistics, just in 2010 the French gendarmerie and police registered 10,000 complaints of rape. It is estimated that this number corresponds to just 10 percent of the total number of actual rapes. In reality, at least 75,000 women are raped every year, corresponding to 200 rapes a day. This means that in France every sixth woman is raped over her lifetime. In addition to actual acts of rape, there are annually 198,000 attempted rapes; 45 percent of rapes occur during the day; 67 percent in the home of the victim or the perpetrator; 51 percent cause bodily harm.

---

49 See www.journaldesfemmes.com.

50 An article published in *The Economist* magazine on July 20, 2013 reported that the level of crime is dropping in all of the wealthy countries except for the United States and France. The causes given included an aging population, the increase in the rate of incarceration, a decrease in the use of cash, a higher level of video surveillance and the creation of private security services.

This problem is not unique to France: in Italy, 4.3 percent of women say that they have been raped at least once in their lives;[51] In England and Wales 85,000 women are raped every year.[52] In 2006 in the United States 207,754 people were victims of sexual violence;[53] 5,000 in Sweden; 635 in Switzerland. Every day in South Africa 147 women are raped, mostly in poor city neighborhoods. In Belgium every year 3,000 rapes are registered, of which between 230 and 300 are gang-rapes.[54]

In France, according to ONDRP,[55] every year 278,000 people become victims of sexual crimes, while 7 percent of French women say that they have been raped. Just 2 percent of the rapes result in punishment for the perpetrator.

Also according to ONDRP, every day there are 6,000 crimes committed against property, 1,300 cases of violence against persons, 1,000 cases of fraud in the economic and financial spheres. Every day in France 470 cars are destroyed or damaged. Every day sees 330 murders or attempted murders in the course of a mugging, and 100 cases of arson are investigated. In 2005, 3,755,000 cases of thefts were registered, compared with 187,000 in 1950,[56] 1,233,000 in 1975 and 2,302,000 in 1985. ONDRP estimates that these numbers are just the tip of the iceberg, and that in reality the number of these crimes is three times higher.

---

51 *Statistiche in breve—Famiglia e società*. ISTAT, 2006.
52 *An overview of sexual offending in England and Wales*. Ministry of Justice, Office for National Statistics, Home Office, 2013.
53 United States Department of Justice, 2006.
54 Ministry of Internal Affairs of Belgium, 2011.
55 National service for crime and criminal punishment.
56 Of course, the population was smaller in 1950. Still, such a dramatic jump is quite shocking.

For multiple reasons (deteriorating schools and social systems, breakups of families, withdrawal of the state and the powers of law and order) over 20 years the crime rate in France has increased by 20-fold, while the jail population has increased only fourfold. Only a few criminals ever see the inside of a jail. Impunity? A lax justice system? In his book *France: A Clockwork Orange*,[57] Laurent Obertone quips: "Aggression can be called free, because the aggressor never pays!"

There is also a resurgence of such deplorable acts as assaults against honor and dignity, forced marriages, polygamy, genital mutilation, appearance of hitherto unheard-of phenomena such as "happy slapping"[58] and harassment with the use of violence.[59]

Such crises are at the same personal and social, and although they can touch anyone, according to the statistics the ones who suffer from them most are women.

Local, regional, national crises

Depending on where we live, we are exposed to a smaller or greater risk of catastrophes that can ruin the day for us and our neighbors: floods, hurricanes, forest fires, cold snaps, heat waves, tornados, earthquakes, volcanic eruptions, tsunami, viral epidemics and incidents of severe environmental contami-

---

57 Obertone L., *La France: Orange Mécanique*, 2012.

58 In these incidents one person suddenly starts beating a pedestrian while another films the event, then posts the video on the internet or sells it illegally. Sometimes the beatings escalate into murder or rape. Psychologists consider this phenomenon one of the manifestations of rivalry between youth gangs—*Editor's note*.

59 See www.spi0n.com/la-drague-du-93-par-une-claque.

nation. These are risks of sanitary, natural, social (unrest) catastrophes, as well as technological catastrophes: nuclear (Chernobyl, Fukushima), industrial (Bhopal,[60] Toulouse). All of these can seriously afflict our life and the lives of our families.

Aside from the possibility of dying or being grievously harmed in such catastrophes, there is also the risk of temporary or permanent loss of the ability to live in one's home. In addition to all sorts of discomforts and privations, this can result in the loss of our possessions which have both a material and a psychological value, the latter of which no insurance company and no social assistance can replace.

Although these risks may be small relative to the risk of a crisis on a personal level, we must concede that they can have devastating effects on our familiar environment.

Cyclones Lothar and Martin in 1999: 91 dead, 200 toppled high-voltage pylons in France, and as a result over 3 million families remained without electricity for several days.

The 2001 explosion at the AZF factory in Toulouse killed 31 and wounded 2,500. A year and a half after the explosion almost 14,000 people were still in treatment, suffering from insomnia, anxiety and depression.

Hurricane Katrina in the United States in 2005: 1,836 dead, 135 missing, 3 million houses left without electricity for several weeks. This incident has created the largest diaspora in US history, numbering over a million people who were forced to leave their homes and neighborhoods. The economic damage

---

60 An accident at the American chemical factory in Bhopal (India) is considered the largest technogenic catastrophe in modern history in terms of the number of victims—18,000 people died, 150,000-600,000 injured.

has been calculated to be over 150 billion dollars.

Cyclone Xynthia in 2010: 54 dead, extreme coastal flooding, over a million people left without electricity.

Hurricane Sandy in 2012: at least 286 dead on Caribbean islands and in North America. In New York, all airports were closed, as well as the main hospitals, public transportation and the stock exchange.

Flooding in Europe from the end of May to the beginning June 2013, especially in Germany (Thuringia, Saxony, Bavaria, Baden-Würtemberg), Czech Republic, Austria and the southwest of France, resulted in the death of several tens of people, a serious crisis in the distribution of consumer goods and huge physical damage.

The anomalously cold winter in January and February of 2014 in the United States.

Public unrest in France in 2005, In the United Kingdom in 2011, in Sweden in 2013...

Convergence of crises and economic collapse

We see it as increasingly probable that the convergence of negative tendencies, each of which alone would bring on a crisis, will cause a global economic collapse, because of the fragility inherent in our contemporary world discussed in the previous chapter.

What are these negative tendencies?

The rapid increase in the total population of the earth, which grew from two to seven billion people in less than a hundred years, has continued in spite of declining birth rates. These seven, soon to be eight billion people will be attempting to feed themselves, dress themselves, obtain housing, send their children to school and, in keeping with the Western model, own cars, televisions and eat meat. This exponential increase in the rate of consumption not only requires large expenditures, but also causes problems that must be taken into account.

Pollution caused by human activity poses a threat to marine and terrestrial ecosystems on which our life depends, and they are collapsing one after another: the oceans are emptying of life, the forests are becoming deforested, the soils are being depleted and losing their biological diversity—and these are only some of the consequences. This is rapidly reducing the Earth's ability to feed a population that is growing both in size and its demands for consumption. A population that cannot satisfy its needs or is experiencing chronic hunger is one of the factors that causes unrest, fanaticism, civil wars and mass migrations. The trouble can be considerable, as shown by the situations in Somalia, former Zaire, Sierra-Leone... among others!

Endless exponential growth of the world economy in a world of finite resources is, by definition, impossible. The greater part of resources (cheap oil, natural gas, coal, rare earth metals,[61] phosphates, fresh water) which we require in order to maintain our lifestyles, are being depleted faster and faster, increase in price, and this will slow down, then stop,

---

61 Rare earth metals are a group of metals that includes scandium, yttrium, lutecium and 12 tantalanoids. They have specific and highly beneficial qualities that allow them to be used in modern technologies, "green" industry (such as the manufacturing of solar panels and hybrid vehicles) and the creation of special alloys and magnets.

then reverse economic growth. In the process, the age-old struggle of people over resources will grow desperate. In this context, we should not rule out the possibility of regional and world wars.

Without economic growth it is impossible to finance the social safety net (pensions, benefits). Without economic growth it is impossible to repay the colossal debts that have been incurred by governments, regional and local administrations, companies and families in order for them to finance their consumption and to create the illusion of wealth without creating genuine wealth.[62]

The modern economic system is becoming ever more financialized and ever more indebted. But the debts have to be repaid sooner or later, and without economic growth this is impossible. Debts can also be repudiated and negotiated down, but then credit dries up, and since our economies run chronic deficits, this would force them to resort to drastic austerity measures, leading to strikes, social unrest and a massive reduction in economic activity. Finally, debt can be eliminated by printing money, thus lowering the value of money, reducing the amount of debt through inflation. This is the method that has been used most often by governments and central

---

62 Consider the meaning of the phrase which was pronounced in 1802 by Thomas Jefferson, when he was the second president of the United States: "I believe that banking institutions are far more dangerous to our freedoms than a multitude of soldiers ready to fight. If the American people ever allows private banks to control its money, the banks and associated institutions will deprive them of their property, first through inflation, then through recession. And this will go on until their children—deprived of house and home—will wake up on the earth conquered by their parents."

banks (and is continuing to be used by Japan, United States, European Union, United Kingdom, Switzerland and other countries). But every time this has been tried, it has driven up prices, sometimes exponentially (in case of hyperinflation) and has always ended up diminishing the amount of savings and reducing the purchasing power of the population.[63] Debts are a path to poverty and serfdom.[64]

Without financing, the global economy would not be able to function at a level of efficiency that allows it to remain global-ized, interdependent and "just in time."

The result of the convergence of negative tendencies, more and more probable, is a crisis that begets another crisis, which begets the third, and so on ad infinitum, only increasing the stresses on the complex and fragile system, until eventually something cracks and it collapses.

This has already happened repeatedly and has sometimes led to the disappearance of entire civilizations: the Roman Em-pire, the Maya Empire, the Soviet Union and so on. Unfortu-nately, it is impossible to accurately predict which event, which danger, which uncontrollable factor[65] will let loose one of these crises, but the end result is becoming increasingly un-avoidable: that which we consider to be the "normal" must, by definition, undergo a dramatic change.

---

63 A recent financial innovation is the gradual destruction of debt through negative interest rates. It is at the moment too early to tell what unintended consequences it will have—Editor's note.
64 We took this expression from the title of the famous book by Friedrich von Hayek The Road to Serfdom, published in 1944.
65 See Taleb N. N. The Black Swan: the Impact of the Highly Improbable, 2010.

Are we in denial?

The majority of us keep our nose to the grindstone, worn out from work, shopping, the commute, the bureaucracy, housework, bringing up children and dealing with all the little "crises" of everyday adult life. We don't even want to consider all of the possibilities, the unsettling statistics, the facts and figures that strike fear into our hearts!

Most of the worn-out, overloaded population closes their eyes and takes shelter in denial: "This can't happen to me! This can't happen to me!"

Denial is a perfectly normal psychological defense mechanism. Even though we are all living examples of excellent adaptation to our environment,[66] the comforts of our contemporary world beguile us into ignoring reality, and our denial "defends" us from additional stress.

Our ancestors elevated foresight to the position of an everyday and vitally important need. For example, they created stockpiles of food and managed their households most conservatively. But our foresight—that of modern, highly interdependent people—was eventually supplanted by the strange idea that this is all somebody else's problem.

Somebody else is responsible for feeding us.

Somebody else is responsible for defending us.

Somebody else is responsible for repairing our equipment and houses, and for developing technologies for us to use.

Somebody else...

---

66 In the end, all of us are, by definition, descended from those who managed to survive previous crises.

This break with reality, this denial, in a time when crises are neither products of fantasy nor paranoia, can turn out to be very dangerous.

Let us look at the statistics: fires and traffic accidents affect a family every two minutes; every fifth woman is depressed; every sixth woman is raped over her lifetime; 44 out of every 100 women are divorced; more than 10 percent of those who are looking for work can't find it.

Ecological crises and the obvious depletion of natural resources are confirmed by scientific data. Financial and inflationary crises are attested throughout history. They have happened repeatedly in France, Germany, and most recently in Argentina, Zimbabwe, Russia and Algeria... When it comes to social unrest, revolts, hunger and war, they are all featured daily on our television news programs.

In spite of all the evidence, the vast majority of us stubbornly deny these destabilizing realities. We have been programmed to do so. By now, we are so used to being dependent on the "machine" that we are forced to keep ourselves convinced of its longevity and reliability. We are forced to convince ourselves that our support systems—supply, manufacturing, agriculture—and the economic systems will always be functioning, no matter what, forever.

And this is why we often see the realities of our modern world as spectators, rather than as actors who create their own well-being.

4. Consequences

"I attribute my success to this: I never gave or took any excuse."
—Florence Nightingale, British nurse (1820-1910)

"Worry retards reaction and makes clear-cut decisions impossible."
—Amelia Earhart, aviation pioneer (1897-1937)

No matter the exact nature of a crisis—economic, ecological, natural, political, social, technological, sanitary... and no matter its scale—personal, local, regional, national, global... we must consider its mechanisms and its possible consequences.

We have seen that our economic systems and life support systems are very complex ("just in time," specialization, interdependence).

Such complexity implies great structural vulnerability.

Vulnerability leads to the sudden appearance of possible instability.

In the end, instability means that we can't predict anything.

Consequently, a crisis—a malfunction or a crash of all that which we consider normal—can descend on us at any moment and destabilize the balance, the homeostasis[67] of our home life.

Quite often this destabilization is short in duration and does not significantly affect us. But sometimes the effects can be more serious—all the way to the destruction of the economic and social base upon which rests the sum total of our modern world.

And it can lead to shortages.

The shortages result from all of the innate, atavistic, regressive human impulses, such as fear, despair, panic, violence...

However, we can observe that in the case of each crisis—be it loss of work, a personal economic crisis, cut-off of the water supply, a natural disaster (hurricane Katrina in New Orleans in 2005; tsunami in Japan in 2011...), civil war (Bosnia, Rwanda) or economic collapse (the USSR, Argentina, Zimbabwe...)—each of us reacts differently to the resulting unhappiness, stress and tension.

We react differently because our reactions are conditioned by our culture, the sum total of all the acquaintances we have accumulated throughout our lives, the quantity and quality of our material resources, but most importantly by our own, unique personal needs.

But all of have the same fundamental needs, which are inseparable from our need to live. All of us need to breathe,

---

67 To remind: homeostasis is the ability of a system to maintain a dynamic equilibrium in spite of external forcing.

drink, eat, sleep and maintain optimal body temperature. These biological needs are essential to our survival, and exist in parallel with psychological and psycho-social needs, such as security, love and belonging.

Self-actualization	morality creativity spontaneity problem-solving lack of prejudice acceptance of facts
Esteem	self-esteem, confidence, achievement, respect for others, respect by others
Love/Belonging	friendship, family, sexual intimacy
Safety	security of body, of employment, of resources, of morality, of the family, of health, of property
Physiological	breathing, food, water, sex, sleep, homeostasis, excretion

This hierarchy of needs is often shown as the Maslow[68] pyramid, shown above.

Today, in the center of the contemporary world, our needs are more important than ever. Psychologists and sociologists regularly add layers to the pyramid in order to reflect our latest needs.

---

68 Abraham Harold Maslow, 1908-1970, American psychologist. He is considered the father of humanistic psychology, and is well-known as the author of this pyramid of needs.

Let us mention some of these new needs: a safe working environment, high-quality and universally accessible education, high-quality housing, all the necessary medical services, an unpolluted environment, stable economics... Although these needs would have seemed excessive to the denizens of London's commercial waterfront in the 18th century,[69] or to Parisians of the Middle Ages, today we consider them existentially important to our lives...

But our quest for comfort and new technologies does not stop at more or less justifiable sociopolitical considerations. We must note that along with our instinct to always want more of everything, and under the influence of advertising and political propaganda of the governments, modern marketing has invaded our lives, giving us the illusion of ever greater, inordinately huge needs that sometimes seem quite ridiculous.

Examples?

Our houses, and each of the rooms, is becoming ever bigger; our diet is ever more varied and exotic (strawberries in winter?) and ever higher in calories; our cars are ever more luxurious and powerful. The per capita use of water, electricity and crude oil is constantly increasing. Various computerized devices and gadgets (monitors, computers, telephones and so on) are becoming ever more widespread, require ever more frequent replacement, and create ever greater levels of dependency. And then there's baconnaise![70]

---

69 During that time 50 percent of the female population of London (and other European cities, be it Dublin or Naples) had to engage in prostitution in order to be able to survive.

70 Baconnaise is bacon-flavored mayonnaise made by the company J&D Foods. It is a mixture of mayonnaise, fried pork fat and salt.

The thing is... the greater our needs, the more dependent we are on the smooth functioning of our immediate environment in order to maintain our lifestyles. In the end, it was just this problem that the dinosaurs encountered 60 million years ago—the largest ones, with the largest dietary needs. They were the ones to disappear first. In the meantime, the smallest dinosaurs[71] and the small mammals, whose needs were minimal, survived "the end of the world" of their epoch.

And so, when this dynamic of codependence is overturned by the consequences of a crisis, we are faced with the reality of our primary needs, in the order of their vital necessity for our continued existence, but also in light of our understanding of what is actually necessary. A woman living in a Brazilian favela, who is used to getting by on very little, will not be blindsided by a shortage, in stark contrast to the inhabitant of posh neighborhoods of Zurich, Malibu or Neuilly-sur-Seine, who are known to complain loudly if once a year electricity goes out for 10 minutes, or if their driver is slightly late.

To illustrate the tight connection between our needs and the consequences of a crisis, here are some specific examples which underscore the necessity to prepare, on an individual, family, neighborhood and group level, to satisfy our primary needs—to respond to those of our needs which are the primary ones—the most urgent, the most essential and the most important.

---

71 Ancestors of birds.

Hurricane Sandy

On October 28, 2012 hurricane Sandy ravaged the eastern seaboard of the United States, striking especially hard the states of New York, New Jersey and Maryland.

During the very first hours of Sandy's impact, highways were closed because of heavy snow showers. Many roads became blocked and impassable due to fallen trees and utility poles. Sewer systems overflowed, creating a huge sanitary danger. Air transport was disrupted by hurricane-force winds, and nuclear power stations were shut down because of numerous faults with the electric grid. Ports and water terminals were blocked because of huge waves and storm surges. Highway and railroad tunnels were closed due to flooding. Train traffic stopped because of the flooding of rail corridors and reserve generators. The majority of commercial and industrial enterprises were closed. Electric transformer explosions and natural gas leaks caused fires...

In all, approximately 6.2 million houses were deprived of electricity.[72] Repairs to the electric grid went on, on average, for eight days. No fewer than 210 people died, and 20 people disappeared without a trace. The hurricane cased the United States more than 50 billion dollars in damage.

What were the direct consequences?

Millions of people, millions of contemporary families with their very considerable needs were suddenly deprived of electricity, heat, sometimes of water and fuel, having come directly face to face with the vulnerability of their life support

---

72 See http://www.usatoday.com/story/weather/2012/10/29/hurricane-sandy-east-coast-frankenstorm/1666105.

systems.

The National Guard and specialized government organizations such as FEMA[73] had to intervene massively in order to rescue people who had lost their shelter and to distribute emergency aid: drinking water, food, blankets, medicines... In spite of their efforts, the aid was clearly insufficient.

In reality, difficulties with the distribution system soon became the main problem. The oil terminals of the region suffered considerable damage, and seven of them remained closed for several weeks. Breaks in electric transmission lines resulted in the shutdown of pipelines which delivered refined petroleum products from the Gulf of Mexico to the oil terminals in New Jersey. According to data from the US Department of Energy, on November 9 28 percent of the gas stations in New York were still out of fuel. Fuel rationing was introduced, and policemen were stationed at each gas station in order to maintain order. The limits were lifted on November 17 on Long Island and on November 24 in all of New York. The majority of cities and towns along the Atlantic coast were flooded. Hundreds of houses were condemned and demolished, not counting hundreds of others that were already partially or completely destroyed by fire, wind or water.

Before the hurricane made landfall, Marie, a young French woman who was spending her vacation in New York, said in an interview to the radio station Europe 1 that she was extremely surprised when crowds of people ran to supermarkets and emptied the shelves: "When my friends told me that I should lay in supplies, I thought that they were being a bit paranoid. Really, it was strange to see everyone standing in line. It was as

---

73 Federal Emergency Management Agency.

if we were in a war."

Well before hurricane Sandy descended on New York, long before its serious consequences connected with flooding and structural damage were felt, the population went into shock when it realized how quickly all of the essential products disappeared from store shelves: water, food, flashlights, medications, diapers, feminine sanitary products, pet food, candles, gasoline, garbage bags, portable heaters, tents, sleeping bags, blankets, plastic containers, lighters, matches, work gloves, rope... million of people suddenly and simultaneously experienced the lack of these basic products.

As we have already said, the fragility of the systems of distribution and support based on "just in time" principles, specialization and interdependency leads to a situation where our normality depends mainly on the uninterrupted supply of huge retail spaces, local stores, hospitals, gas stations, pharmacies... using road, water and air transport.

In a period of crisis, people understand—or, rather, feel— that the situation will very quickly cause a certain disequilibrium, either because the demand for essential products will outstrip their supply, or because the crisis will create impediments to their distribution.

And since the majority of contemporary families also live according to "just in time" principles, as Marie observed in New York during hurricane Sandy, supermarkets and commercial centers are immediately emptied of products and cut off from their warehouses.

Another consequence of hurricane Sandy was that millions of families suddenly lost access to electricity. And although the average length of repairs to the electric grid was eight days, in reality in certain neighborhoods it took more than four weeks.

Potentially, depending on the severity of this or that calamity, it may entail four weeks without refrigerators, light, radio, television, computers, coffeemakers, electric space heaters, washers and driers, dishwashers, fans, heat, elevators, telephones, running water and—what horror!—without wifi.

This is nothing special for families that are organized and prepared to return to the 18th century with their sense of humor, peace of mind and joie de vivre intact... but imagine what it's like for elderly people, for people with limited abilities, vulnerable people, people living on the seventh floor of a high-rise building, sick and lonely people, and all those who completely depend on the smooth functioning of the contemporary machine in order to continue to live!

The electric grid is often the first systematic casualty of such natural disasters as hurricane Sandy. But it is this particular life-support system, so vulnerable and fragile, that is beyond all doubt the very basis for the normal functioning of a multitude of more or less existentially important bits and pieces of our modern society. The problem is that the "electric fairy" has become our first and main necessity, the "goddess" underpinning our modern world.

Gas pumps, hospitals, streetlights, transportation, refrigerators, the banking system, the internet, communications of all kinds, security services, pumped water... all of these systems depend on the normal functioning of the electric grid. This is especially important in the cities, where the dependency of the population has a more obvious, tangible character than in rural areas.

Spending 24 hours in the dark is not so horrible an experience in and of itself, but if on top of that you are deprived of water and heat for several weeks, in a city of several million, it turns into a horrific ordeal.

The healthcare system is also extremely vulnerable during local and regional shocks, but most importantly during the worst case scenario—a national or a global catastrophe.

This vulnerability is clearly illustrated whenever the need suddenly comes to exceed the overall capabilities of the health care infrastructure: hospitals, clinics, treatment centers, pharmacies, and also pharmaceutical factories, research centers, epidemiological laboratories and so on. Health care delivery infrastructure obviously includes the hospitals themselves, but it also includes everything that provides for their functioning at an optimal level: pharmacists, emergency medical technicians, lab workers, nurses, doctors, surgeons, anesthesiologists, maintenance workers, kitchen staff... All of them play an important role in helping the sick. The hospital universe is entirely dependent on complex subsystems, such as the electric grid, the public water supply, transportation and communications.

On October 29, less than 24 hours after hurricane Sandy descended on the coast, two hundred patients of the Langone Medical Center at NYU were placed under evacuation orders. Bellevue, Cony Island and the Palisades Medical Center, all of which are absolutely vital for the residents of these areas, were either partially or totally evacuated.

The main reason for the evacuations was a power outage, which had happened immediately, along with flooding and logistical problems (lack of fuel) and the inability to start electrical generators. If access to electric power only rarely plays a vital role for private individuals, it is crucially important to the smooth functioning of hospitals and to their most vulnerable patients.

To these vital problems we should add a lack of staff, many of whom failed to show up for work, along with an immediate surge in requests for help (from wounded, elderly and lonely people, refugees, the homeless and so on). Here we encounter one of the factors that is a constant in a criss: systematic diffi‐ culties encountered by health care systems, which are unable to function in situations that deviate from the norm.

Emergency responders such as ambulances, fire brigades and more specialized rescue units also function badly in times of natural disaster: due to impassable roads, communications system outages, too dangerous a working environment or weather that keeps helicopters grounded... In an emergency, we can quickly lose access to professional services.

If a medical emergency is a source of stress and anxiety even when all is well, the inability to call for help (because the phones are out) or to quickly go to the hospital (roads closed, no fuel...) inevitably results in a dramatic situation.

Here is what Olivia Yan, resident of Hoboken, New Jersey, told journalists from the TV channel TF1: "We followed our safety instructions, which advised us to stockpile food, in par‐ ticular, to lay in a supply of drinking water to last a few days." She added: "We filled all the containers we had, in order to have water for various needs. Then we froze in anticipation, knowing that the night will be difficult... Many people rein‐ forced their windows with sticky tape, so that the glass wouldn't shatter, as we were advised to do."

During hurricane Sandy the residents of new York quickly lost access to cable television and the internet—which was like the end of the world! They also lost access to mobile phone service, which in our times is an essential service, both on the individual and the professional level. Sell phone service failed from overloading, caused by countless people trying to warn, alert, reassure and encourage each other, and, later, from their inability to charge their batteries. For many days land line phones and public phones were the only reliable methods of communication for the majority of New York's inhabitants.

The partial or complete loss of communications greatly affected the work of teams responsible for the organization of aid, support and supply. For example, hospitals could not get in touch with specialists in order to consult them concerning the treatment of patients who suffered from particular types of wounds. Security services also had great difficulty in coordinating the activities of their teams, which found themselves without cell phones and with no ability to charge their portable radios.

As was reported in New York Daily News, after hurricane Sandy descended on Queens, this peninsula has turned into a kingdom of crime, where the police are even more scarce than electricity and food.

Although most of the residents who experienced the after-effects of Sandy handled them through mutual aid and solidarity, calmly standing in line in front of food trucks, helping their neighbors and volunteering in the repair and clean-up of the affected neighborhoods, nevertheless, just as with hurricane Katrina in 1995, New York and the surrounding areas saw widespread thefts, burglaries and acts of violence.

In extreme situations, such as hurricane Sandy, the increase in criminal behavior becomes a reality with which we have to cope whether we want to or not. Security which, according to Maslow, is one of our foremost needs, along with water, food and normal body temperature, leaps to the foreground. Without it we are unable to provide for our own physical well-being, or the well-being of those close to us, or to safeguard supplies and belongings that are vital to our survival.

The causes for the increase in crime are often connected with a convergence of many factors. These factors more or less quickly cause a collapse in morality, blunt the feelings of compassion and fairness, and, at a greater scale, destroy public order. Our social veneer, our civilizational superego, just is the rest of our modernity, is complex, and, consequently quite fragile.

The first factor which affects the quality of information and, in consequence, the stability of crime rates, is often loss of electricity. Without electricity streets and dwellings go dark, emergency call boxes stop working, along with video surveillance equipment and, most importantly, contact with security services is lost.

The second factor is connected in some measure with the herd instinct, and with the loss of self-control. Certain individuals suddenly perceive the emergency situation as a free-for-all—a chance to rob, assault and pillage with complete impunity.

The third factor is the partial or complete collapse of public order. Events can quickly disrupt the work of security services, which often become physically unable to respond to calls for help (because of disruptions in communication systems, impassable roads, broken vehicles, priority given to the defense of public buildings and VIPs, inability to get to work, etc.)

Whether we speak of financial collapse in Argentina or Greece, the earthquake in Haiti, the siege of Sarajevo, social unrest or natural disasters, a citizen can, against her will, find herself in a situation where she is forced, first and foremost, to care about her own security and physical and psychological well being, and those of the people near to her.

Unrest in the French suburbs in 2005

The civil unrest and rioting of 2005 started on October 27 in Clichy-sous-Boi, then quickly spread to other communities in France and continued until November 17, when the police declared that the situation has returned to normal. The main targets of the rioters were security services, public transport, commercial and industrial zones that were called upon to supply with work the inhabitants of the so-called "people's" neighborhoods, as well as educational institutions. Several hundred youths did not hesitate to arm themselves with Molotov cocktails, and they threw stones, washing machines and anything else at hand at the representatives of security services.

In all, over 10,000 cars were burned, along with numerous public buildings, schools, kindergartens and nurseries; chain stores were looted.

These three weeks of criminality run wild were the largest single incident of unrest in France since the events of May 1968. They were stunning not just in their duration but in the scale of destruction throughout France, as well as in their previously unheard of level of coverage in the mainstream media. Similar incidents of unrest erupted in the United Kingdom in 2011 and in Sweden in 2013.

A report from Central directorate for general information,[74] dated November 23 and published in the newspaper *Le Parisien* on December 7, 2005, states: "France has encountered a form of disorganized rebellion, which coincided in time and space with public manifestations in population centers which lacked a leader or a program. No solidarity between the population centers could be observed; youths identified themselves by their belonging to their native neighborhoods and did not recognize those from other communities. No evidence has been uncovered of any manipulation, which would allow us to speak of a general, organized revolt."

The police stated that "the youth of population centers possessed a strong identifying sentiment, based not just on their ethnic or geographic origins, but on their social position as outcasts from French society." They specify that "the youth of problematic neighborhoods felt itself to be oppressed due to poverty, skin color and names. Those who looted the cities had in common lack of hopes for the future and ability to find employment in French society. Everything happened as if trust has been lost, and not just in public institutions but also in the private sector—the source of envy, jobs and economic integration."

This unrest and its aftermath cost France 200 million euros. The populations of the affected neighborhoods and communities suffered the most, and not just in a material, but also in a psychological sense: people started to be afraid to leave their

74 *Direction Centrale des Renseignements Généraux.*

homes. The main problem became the lack of security, not lack of food.

Fatima, a resident of Aulnay-sous-Bois, said that although during the time of unrest the shops in her neighborhood were closed, she could leave her neighborhood, on foot or by car, in order to shop and to fill up the gas tank. She said: "Most of all I feared that somebody on the street will suddenly attack me or my children. Mass media blew the events out of all proportion, pouring oil on the fire, and after that various bands started to compete in violence. As soon as I was able, I left the neighborhood, because the bands were becoming more and more cruel, and it was all closely connected with organized crime... drugs, weapons, women..."[75]

The majority of the population of these neighborhoods, consisting of honest citizens, asked itself: What would happen if one day the state, due to budget cuts or lack of resources associated with the economic crisis and the large government debt, would stop maintaining law and order?

Individual Financial Crisis

These days in Western countries more and more households have started to feel the onset of an individual financial crisis. An economy that is barely growing, the inability of the political elite to solve any problems at all, austerity, lay-offs and companies going out of business...

What are the consequences? They are: unemployment, curtailment of government assistance, cuts to pensions, inflation that destroys the value of savings, bursting real estate bubbles,

---

75 In an interview with the author.

stock market crashes, increases in the prices of essential products, difficulties in meeting basic needs in food and medicine, depression and anxiety, increases in tension between family members resulting in costly divorces... and, unfortunately, numerous suicides among those faced with such oppressive economic adversity.

Ask yourself the following questions:

- What would you do if you and your family became victims of an economic catastrophe? Do you have a plan of action? Do you have an emergency plan? An exit plan? The means to offer resistance, to overcome difficulties, and to rebuild?
- What would you do if you lose your income? What if you lose your job during a situation that is unstable bordering on disastrous, such as occurred after the collapse of the Soviet Union, Argentina, or in an economic situation such as in Greece at this very moment?
- What will you do if your salary, unemployment benefits or pension are cut in half? How about by two-third? What would happen if the payments stopped altogether?
- For how long would you be able to continue paying rent, mortgage and real estate taxes once you are left without earnings or public assistance?
- For how long would you be able to continue to pay taxes on your land once your income is gone?
- For how long would you able to continue to eat, dress yourself, pay for transportation, pay for electricity, water and heat, once you are left without earnings or pub-

lic assistance?

- What will you do if food prices and other resources, such as electricity, natural gas or gasoline, start going up by 300 percent every month? How about 600 percent?
- What would you do if you couldn't afford a nanny or a baby-sitter?
- If you don't work, what would you do if your spouse, the breadwinner of the family, suffers an accident, loses employment, becomes seriously ill or dies suddenly?
- Do you have a plan in case of economic collapse—at the scale of the family, the country, or the world?

Do you find such questions melodramatic and exaggerated?

Well then, look around you! The number of people and families who can barely make ends meet every month, sink into debt and are left without work, is steadily climbing. We are speaking of individuals who are slowly falling into an economic abyss due to their excessive consumption, in the name of endless economic growth, or because of an emergency in the family, or of entire peoples who are afflicted by the economic collapse of their countries. These days, economic catastrophe is, unfortunately, turning into a commonplace, palpable reality.

The consequences of this economic erosion at a personal, national or global scale can take different forms and be expressed in different ways; for example, through the appearance of tent cities in the United States, especially in California, where thousands of families, having encountered more or less sudden economic problems, have been forced to live in tents or garden sheds. The example of California is quite interesting, because this state occupies eighth place in the rankings of the world's economies. This is a very wealthy region, but today's extreme economic situation is striking even at social classes whose members just yesterday owned houses of 200 square meters[76] and two cars, living in quite comfortable circumstances that to them seemed that they would last forever. To spend many years traveling first class, and then to suddenly find yourself stuffed not even in second class but in the baggage compartment—that is by no means a joyous perspective!

Consequences in Everyday Life

These events are only a small part of the tragedies experienced by the millions of victims of natural and humanitarian catastrophes which occur every year throughout the world. These events, which are in principle local and short-lived, seem insignificant in comparison to such long-term calamities as the Great Depression which set in after the collapse of 1929.

"The state of war" which Marie hinted at when she told of supermarkets in New York, is, in the final analysis, just a consequence of our own mismanagement and our adherence to the principle of "just in time" in running our households. This "state of war" would not have arisen, or would have been less severe, if only everyone had at least a ten-day supply of vital resources (water, food, energy, products for personal hygiene...).

---

76 Just over 2000 square feet.

It is interesting to note that the expression "to stockpile" is often cast in a negative light, as if this practice—old-fashioned, natural and logical—in some fundamental way contradicts healthy, balanced social behavior... and is somehow incompatible with "altruistic" behavior.

But a normal stockpile of essential necessities adapted to the needs of the family can by itself contribute to lessening numerous problems associated with shortages and unforeseen emergencies. Among such problems we can count the possibility of becoming victims of acts and situations that are chaotic, dangerous, alarming and even tragic. That was just the situation of the people who took shelter at the Superdome in New Orleans during hurricane Katrina. A similar situation was seen in the sudden jump in the number of suicides in 2011 in Japan after the tsunami. And all of this in spite of the fact that our governments regularly exhort us to be prepared for emergency situations. All we have to do is follow their advice.

What do our governments recommend?

Numerous branches of government persistently encourage their citizens to maintain a minimal level of preparation, to stock up on certain supplies (food, medications, water, emergency funds...) and goods (blankets, fuel, candles, batteries, a first aid kit...) and to prepare for the possibility that they will be unable to satisfy their needs.

Here is a sample of what certain governments recommend, so as to avoid being caught entirely unawares:

In the United States, FEMA[77] has developed an emergency alert system for regions of North America and dispenses useful advice, distributing detailed lists of items that should go into one's emergency kit, to be used in case of a crisis: food, water, tools, clothes. Its motto is: "Gather your emergency kit, make a plan and stay informed!"

In France there exists an Interministerial Portal for the mitigation of major risks.[78] The goal of the portal is to explain, based on examples, the behavior which individuals, families and companies should adopt during crises and periods of major risk (floods, heat waves, cold snaps, forest fires, tsunamis, earthquakes, volcanic eruptions, pandemics, industrial and nuclear accidents, cyberattacks and so on). From this site we can download a very complete guide on how we should prepare for extreme situations, advice on developing a personal emergency plan, as well as a list of items for an emergency evacuation kit.

In Switzerland, where preparing the population for catastrophes and wars is something of a tradition, the Federal Office for the Economic Welfare of the Country (OFAFE)[79] publishes a guide containing its recommendations. Here is one example: "You should have at home nine liters of water per person, food for at least one week, a portable radio, a pocket flashlight with spare batteries..."

In Québec, "Civil Security"[80] gives advice on how to keep your family safe in case of a natural disaster such as a wind-

---

77 See www.fema.gov.
78 See www.risques.gouv.fr.
79 See www.bwl.admin.ch/dokumentation/00439/index.html?lang=fr.
80 See www.msp.gouv.qc.ca/securite-civile.html.

storm, contamination of drinking water, a blackout...

Belgium has created a General Directorate Crisis Center (DGCC).[81] It helps the government to plan and coordinate the work of departments in crisis situations. Its web site disseminates information, warnings of emergencies and documentation (guides for certain crises, plans for forming volunteer brigades and so on).

The Red Cross,[82] on its international site and on the sites of its regional and local branches, publishes information about administering first aid, to oneself and to other victims, during sanitary emergencies, epidemics, catastrophes and so on.

If it is obvious even to our governments that too heavy a dependence on interconnected and specialized systems working on "just in time" principles carries serious risks for satisfying our vital needs, and if it is clear to us that the complexity of our contemporary world increases the possibility of crises and collapse, then all of us should accept it as evident that constructing our individual realm along the lines of autonomy and stability can only increase our quality of life.

But what does "autonomy" mean these days?

---

81 See www.centredecrise.be.
82 See www.cicr.org/fre.

5. Autonomy

"Begin somewhere. You cannot build a reputation on what you intend to do."
—Liz Smith, British actress

"A desire presupposes the possibility of action to achieve it; action presupposes a goal which is worth achieving."
—Ayn Rand, American writer (1905-1982)

"Integrate what you believe in every single area of your life. Take your heart to work and ask the most and best of everybody else, too."
—Merril Streep, American actress

George Orwell's *1984*, *Brave New World* by Aldous Huxley, *The Age of Limits* by Serge Latouche, *Toward Happy Sobriety* by Pierre Rabhi, *Too Much Magic* by James Howard Kunstler, *Shock Doctrine* by Naomi Klein, *Manufacturing Consent* by Noam Chomsky... all of these books describe something called "anti-utopias" and their implications for our modern world.

Topsoil depletion, shortages of drinking water, massive pollution, climate change, population explosion, resource depletion, Peak Oil, geopolitical conflicts, rampant urbanization, overconsumption, aging infrastructure, privatization of freshwater resources, banking speculations, unrepayable government and private debts, wars, hyperinflation, industrial accidents and technogenic catastrophes, social unrest, civil wars, dictatorship, extremism, epidemics, sanitary and natural catastrophes... the list is as long as it is terrifying!

If we are conscious of the complexities of all of these phenomena, and if we try to preserve the natural environment and quality of life we plan to bequeath to future generations, our task may seem huge, overwhelming. Where do we start looking, starting today, for strategies and solutions that can favorably affect our own well-being and that of those close to us?

That is why it is so important never to stop at simple ideas. At the individual and family level "autonomy" can mean the intention to gain, for an extended period of time, your independence, your self-sufficiency, your stability and, in the final analysis, your freedom.

We are talking about restoring the logical connection between us and the realities of our immediate environment. We are talking about making us the only owners of our lives, nothing more and nothing less.

According to its strictest definition, autonomy signifies our ability to satisfy all of our physiological and psycho-social needs by ourselves.

Obviously, it is impossible to completely fulfill such a utopian vision of self-sufficiency. Nevertheless, I think that we can strive for such autonomy, guided by our intention to reduce as much as possible our level of dependence in areas either too restrictive or too vast.

Specifically, autonomy is, first and foremost, an ideal that can be defined as **our capacity to directly or indirectly influence our complex relationships of dependence/independence**.

This capacity can be realized in practice at the level of the individual, the family, a small community or an entire nation, in many vitally important areas, such as:

Autonomy in **food**, which can be achieved by practicing agriculture, animal husbandry, fishing, hunting, gathering and trade based on mutuality in local, short supply chains.

Autonomy in **energy**, which can be achieved, or planned for, by reducing the use of energy and by working toward greater energy efficiency in using renewable, ecologically benign and long-lived technology: solar and geothermal energy, heat exchangers, etc.

Economic autonomy, in refusing to go into debt, in reducing our needs and expenditures, in changes to the character of our consumption and in relying, for example, on the concepts of microfinance.

Autonomy in **freshwater**: in harvesting rainwater, in fencing in of springs, in digging wells.

Physical autonomy: watching your health, remaining mobile, adhering to principles of self-defense—that is, understanding your responsibility, being vigilant and acting in anticipation.

Autonomy in **everyday life,** based on the principle of "do-it-yourself" (DIY), which can be achieved in many areas: the kitchen, carpentry, mechanics, electricity, sanitation. We can also add refurbishing, remodeling and repair of equipment, tools, furniture and so on.

None of this is particularly new.

For example, more and more architects and urban planners are developing plans for building passive solar houses[83], creating "ecological neighborhoods," including concepts for entire cities[84] that are more and more self-sufficient and capable of producing their own energy, of limiting or reprocessing their own wastes and of offering their residents a more humane environment. We can state that more and more inhabitants of our cities, for a variety of reasons, are discovering for themselves and starting to engage in farming as an additional source of food, to develop family and community gardens, kitchen gardens, to raise chickens and livestock. This was quite typical before the 1960s.

In principle, autonomy is possible in all areas in which we can develop self-sufficiency and are connected to our vital needs (water, food, shelter, hygiene, health) and with our more advanced needs (energy, knowledge) as well as with our skills and lifestyle (individual security, economy, social connections).

---

83 Passive solar houses use solar energy, thermal radiation from household equipment and body heat of the residents to dramatically decrease their need for heating fuel.

84 See, for example, the Masdar project in Abu-Dhabi, in the United Arab Emirates, or, on a smaller scale, the ecological neighborhood of EVA-Lanxmeer in the city of Cuelemborg in the Netherlands.

The path to achieving autonomy is potentially quite wide, and can influence all aspects of our daily life. If we walk that path with intelligence, then, in the long term, it will allow us to lower our expenditures, to create a more stable and carefree future, to minimize our impact on the environment, and to maximize the production of healthier foods.

In contrast to some deplorable deviation from the norm, such efforts in search of autonomy can give us the means to withstand the blows, to escape from crisis, to help others, to alleviate the suffering of others. This will give us resilience,[85] not just at the scale of the family, but also at the scale of the neighborhood, the region, or the country.

Conceptions of Autonomy

For some people the notion of autonomy is associated with regression, of development in reverse, of retreat on the social level, of complete refusal to participate in the system and in modernity. Moreover, incomplete understanding and conceptual confusion reflected in our views, upbringing and cultural endowment can confuse us when we hear of concepts such as survival, voluntary simplicity, decline or autarky.

For certain others—a minority—autonomy offers a way to preempt the effects of a global catastrophe which threatens the survival of our species, and which is sometimes expressed in ways that are grotesque, melodramatic and theatrical: "the end of the world!" This apocalyptic vision, which is often promoted by movies and mass media hungry for sensationalistic

---

85 Here, the term "stability" means the ability of an organism, a community or a structure to adapt to changing circumstances.

content,[86] provides fertile soil for behaviors engendered by paranoia, bunker mentality, conspiracy theories, social militarization, expectation of Armageddon,[87] prophesies, and also ideological, religious and political extremism... No doubt, it is specifically in light of the latter, more sensationalist approach that much of the population has come to see the striving for independence or autonomy: as a fixation on oneself within a Mad Max-like future in which we will be forced to survive with weapons in our hands.

But the reality is that autonomy is not some organized movement defined by precise and absolute rules and protocols. In reality, autonomy has no specific definition that could encompass all the measures taken by this or that person. After all, these measures can be diametrically opposed in their philosophical positions, ultimate objectives, directions, as well as the surrounding situation and the social context in which they evolve.

The ideal of autonomy can be intimately related to the production of natural or ecologically clean food or the concept of limiting economic growth and of embracing voluntary simplicity in both rural and city settings. Autonomy can also be the driver of change and of a total restructuring of the way of life, perhaps with the goal of liberating the rhythm and quality of

---

86 Here we mean Hollywood disaster movies such as *The Road, The Day After Tomorrow, The Postman, Mad Max, 28 Days After, Zardoz, Welcome to Zombieland, Waterworld* and *Planet of the Apes.*

87 Armageddon, from the ancient Hebrew "Mount Meghiddo" is a small mountain in Galilee, in northern Palestine. It is a biblical term mentioned in the New Testament that indicates the place of the final battle between good and evil.

life from dependencies that cannot entirely satisfy one's strivings for independence and freedom.

It is always risky to speak of independence and freedom... These are, on the one hand, relative concepts. On the other hand, we live in an epoch when the striving for independence, self-sufficiency, autonomy, personal power, coherence, participation, serenity, stability and self-esteem can pose a risk for the stability of the dominant economic system that is becoming ever more insistent in pushing us toward ever more dependency.

However, in this increasingly Orwellian context, autonomy is a symbolic reflection of a special consciousness that expresses the idea of liberation from the system, not by means of its destruction—the way of a child frustrated by her own behavior and her inability to follow the rules of a game—but by creating a parallel, stabilizing and liberating way of life.

No doubt there will be friends and family members, not to mention random internet trolls, who will point fingers at us and mock us, belittling our efforts. Happily, the number of those of us who have come to appreciate the concepts of responsibility and autonomy is continuing to grow.

But quite often it very difficult to set realistic priorities for the work of providing for our well-being, or to define specific stages by which we can create a healthy and comfortable habitat.

The steps recommended below can serve as points of departure for your exploration, which you can then carry out yourselves with the help of various specialists.

How Do We Begin?

The first steps can be taken after some very deep thinking about the main questions, large and small, and more or less inescapable, that concern your life:

- How and where do you want to bring up your children?
- What sort of common experience do you want them to become part of?
- What food do you want to eat?
- What water do you want to drink?
- How do you want to live?
- Where do you want to live?
- Under what conditions?
- What sort of contact with nature or with the city do you want to maintain?
- What is your role within your family unit?
- What is particularly important for you?
- What do you dream of?
- What do you want to learn, build, make with your own hands and... rediscover for yourself?
- How and where do you want to spend your old age?
- How do you imagine your life once you are retired?
- How do you imagine the lives of your children once they are retired?

The answers to these essential questions should serve as your lodestar.

The first stage can take a considerable period of time and demands tranquility and the participation of the people you live with, who depend on you and on whom you depend. Of course, these are all entirely individual parameters. There is no textbook that describes this stage step by step.

Clearly, it is much simpler to gain your independence little by little, by using the logic of always moving forward, defined by your geographic situation, your immediate surroundings and your needs.

A heart attack, a road accident, a fire, a burglary, an attack, a financial crash, debts, loss of employment, illness, loss of your life's partner, conflicts in relationships, insecurity... the priority is always to realistically and adequately appraise the probability of this or that event based on our surroundings and our lifestyle.

Simply put, we are far more likely to become victims of a road accident than of having to survive a meteorite strike while standing atop the Eiffel Tower; it is far more probable that we will be confronted with a difficult divorce than with a global nuclear war.

The high-priority effort is to construct a framework for the various components around which we organize our lives:
- Personal (loss of work, sickness, burglary, accident...)
- Local (failure of the water supply, social unrest...)
- Regional (drought, flood...)
- Global (pandemic, war...)

But we will see that no matter what crises and events that disturb normal life, no matter what personal goals you may have, if you are guided by your quest for autonomy and independence, you will inevitably encounter certain unavoidable elements, which you should think about first of all.

Money, debt and wealth

Ancient folk wisdom tells us that it takes money to wage war.

But money also happens to be essential for having leisure time, for buying things, for paying for education... But what is money?

Economic theory defines money as a unit of accounting and exchange produced by a sovereign state, which serves as a store of value and a medium of exchange, and is based on the trust of its users, who are often represented by the abstract notion of "the market."

To keep things simple, in its most primitive sense, money is payment for labor.

To keep things just as simple, debt is money that has to be returned later. This means that it's future labor, because one has to work in order to earn money (in the form of saved income from wages or a salary).

Therefore, debt is future work.

If the debt becomes too large and impossible to repay, particularly because of interest, which is added to the initial borrowed sum, the debt becomes infinitely extended in time, meaning endless work and endless dependency.

Forever...

Another word for it is slavery.[88]

With these preliminary definitions out of the way, we can now state something interesting: that debt has become the

---

88 In ancient Greece and ancient Rome a citizen who could not repay a debt to his creditor became his slave. See Finley M., *Économie et société en Grèce ancienne*, Paris: Seuil, 1997.

central pillar, the nerve center in the construction and main-tenance of the global and globalized economy. Because debt, which is synonymous with dependency and slavery, burdens governments, communities, companies and individuals, we are forced to recognize that our entire economic system, while quite profitable for a tiny minority of us, is heading toward a dead end.

Really, every year millions of people throughout the world —and all around us—fall into the trap set for them by debt and its consequences.

A purchase on credit—of a refrigerator, television, car, washing machine, vacation—is like an attack on our freedom, our dreams and the well-being of our families. The only rea-sonable conclusion that can be drawn from all this is that in preparing for autonomy, the decision to eliminate all debts must have the highest priority.

The only acceptable sort of debt is one that allows us to possess land. This is because land feeds us and is a promise for the future, and is therefore synonymous with independence and all that is commonly regarded as "wealth of the first or-der."

Because if we possess a piece of land that is more or less productive, with some amount of raw materials and resources, and is more or less useful from a political and strategic angle, we own wealth of the first order.

From this first-order wealth flows second-order wealth, which is all that the land supplies us with (crops, forests, rivers, etc.) and what it holds underneath it (minerals, oil, gas, coal, water, etc.)

Third-order wealth is a relatively recent development. It is defined by a monetary equivalent, which we invest in second-order wealth and, ultimately, in first-order wealth. Third-order wealth can be based on sometimes complex subjectivity, because it is subject to parameters and fluctuations of global markets. Third-order wealth is connected with direct and indirect sources of income from exploiting the earth and from rental income, and also from the financialization of these accumulated revenues in the form of financial capital which is, in turn, connected with investments and capital allocation and, as a consequence, with the creation of markets and exchanges. Over time, as the mechanisms for converting one instance of wealth into another grow more complex, financialization takes on an increasingly virtual and nonmaterial character.

You can no longer see or touch your wealth, put it in the trunk of your car and take it with you if the need arises for you to suddenly leave. No doubt, millions on deposit in a Swiss bank account are today's symbols of wealth. But this wealth is third-order wealth, which tomorrow can disappear, because it is just a string of bits—zeroes and ones—on some server that's part of the global financial system, which is dependent, like the rest, on the smooth functioning of the overall system.

And so, what it means "to be wealthy" depends, to a greater or a lesser extent, on what order of wealth you happen to own —first, second or third. There is absolutely no doubt that, in our quest for independence, the best investment on Earth is the Earth itself.

Shelter

After ownership of the Earth comes ownership of shelter. In the process of switching to a settled way of life, which started several tens of thousands of years ago, everyone—rich or poor, man or woman—first of all strove to find, build or equip some sort of structure that could protect them from the forces of nature (the cold, the heat, rain, snow, wind, sand...), help them maintain normal body temperature (thermoregulation), shield them from predators (predatory animals, enemies...), and also provide them with a base that was conducive to their well-being and development, both physical and psychological.

The main function of this "roof over your head" remains thermoregulation. But in the course of our historical evolution property and registration (the legal right to a residence) became increasingly important. With the appearance of cadastral maps and tax codes the "roof of your head" became property that could be sold, gifted, rented, inherited, and structurally or technologically enhanced. Depending on local regulations, sanitation services could be added to it, or greenhouses, or solar panels.

Today our dwellings are much more than just simple shelter. They have become our kitchens, laundries, bedrooms, studies, libraries, theaters, fortresses, bathhouses, gyms and (thanks to the internet) even conference halls.

But if we look back on its origins, shelter remains a firm foundation of our striving for independence and stability. Our shelter is our main piece of equipment.

The purchase of a house that provides us with natural or artificial advantages, including logistical ones, and that stands on arable and fertile land, is a much greater step than just buying property. It is both a refuge and a means of production intended to assist the owner (or the renter) who is striving for independence and autonomy.

Our priorities regarding the creation of a maximally autonomous and stable dwelling must include the water supply (rainwater collection systems), the general design of a system for intelligent passive solar temperature regulation, the possibility of growing healthy food (grown in one's own orchard or kitchen garden) and the steadfast resolution to defend the inhabitants of the house from surrounding dangers, predators and thieves.

These priorities are by no means new.

Over thousands of years they have served as the basis of any organization of a settled way of life on all continents: a nearby source of water and food, defense from heat and cold, and the creation of a system of security or the use of natural features of the surrounding landscape for defense.

And so the requirements for shelter should be kept quite simple:

- Protection from the elements
- Good thermoregulation
- Proximity to a source of water
- Allows for self-sufficiency in food
- Allows for protection of property and of the inhabitants of the dwelling from attack by wild animals and infringement by people

In my previous books, and specifically in my book *Survive Economic Collapse*, I developed the concept of a Sustainable Autonomous Base (SAB) with the objective of transforming your domicile, whether in town or in a rural location, into a reliable, safe place, where you can put down roots, and which will strengthen your ability to live autonomously, independently and stably. The SAB is founded on seven fundamental points: water, food, hygiene and health, energy, knowledge, defense and social connections. In the context of this discussion, here is a brief introduction to each of these fundamental points:

Water

Water... Life... It's not just for drinking!

To satisfy our basic needs, we need 20-50 liters (5-12 gallons) of drinking water, per person, every day... This includes drinking, hygiene and cooking.

If you add growing plants and animal husbandry, these requirements increase by orders of magnitude!

Directly, an average Western family (two adults, two children and a hamster) can easily use up more than 1,000 liters of water a day!

Indirectly, this number depends on its consumption habits. For example, production of:

- 1 kg of beef requires 15,415 liters of water
- a pair of cotton jeans: 11,000 liters
- 1 kg of rice: 3,000 liters
- 1 kg of wheat: 590 liters
- 1 kg of corn: 450 liters
- 1 liter of beer: 25 liters
- 1 empty plastic water bottle: 1.5 liters

The moral of this is: to save water, eat less but drink more beer!

But seriously, these numbers force us to think of our direct and indirect dependence on systems that supply fresh and potable water.

No mater what might happen, crisis or no crisis, our need for water remains an unchanging physiological constant, which we must take into account if we wish to achieve any sort of independence.

Food

Achieving autonomy in food necessarily involves re-equipping the kitchen and creating a long-term stockpile of nonperishable foodstuffs and a stockpile of foodstuffs you eat regularly. Pursuing autonomy in food is an age-old strategy that allows us to economize (by cooking our own food and by buying in bulk at a discount and buying produce locally when it is in season) and also to become independent from large supply chains and industrial food (the networks of business that sell "food"—products of agribusiness laden with pesticides and chemicals prepared with a large amount of sugar, salt and harmful and toxic substances). Along the way this allows you to reduce your impact on the environment (fewer trips, the use of products that come from nearby, etc.).

All of this allows you to minimize the impact of extreme events such as loss of employment, local unrest or a natural disaster such as hurricane Sandy.

Products that are easy to store and which keep for a long time are: pasta, rice, lentils, semolina, dried beans, preserves (fruit, vegetable, meat or fish), and also sugar, salt, vegetable oil (olive, sunflower, rapeseed), honey, jam... If all of this reminds you of your grandmother's pantry, that's normal!

In addition to laying in supplies that can minimize the consequences of this or that event in the short term, for the long-term it is necessary to gain reliable means of producing your own food: by making your own kitchen garden.

It may be hard to believe, but both in the United States[89] and in the European Union[90] kitchen gardens—in both rural areas and the cities, and often based on the principles of permaculture[91]—have become something of a symbol of guerrilla resistance, and more and more often they are coming under attack from local legislatures which seek to limit them or even outlaw them.

We are living through a transitional period. Our lives have a far more elementary and simplified character than the way they are portrayed in any socioeconomic theories or philosophical discussions about the role of each one of us in society. Control over the seed stock, water, energy and firearms rests at the base of the force employed against us more and more

---

89 See www.huffingtonpost.com/2011/07/08/julic-bass-jail-vegetable-garden_n_893436.html

90 See www.developpementdurable.com/conso/2013/05/16663/fareson-potger-pourrait-devenir-illegal.html

91 Permaculture, or "permanent agriculture" is a combination of practices and ways of thinking directed at creating food production systems that are energy-efficient (in terms of manual labor and fuel) and environmentally safe. Permaculture strives to create a production system for food and other useful resources, leaving as much space as possible for wild nature. It uses ecological concepts, functional design, biological agriculture, among others.

frequently by the government, large pharmaceutical companies and agribusiness concerns. They impact our most fundamental needs, because they reduce our means, our capacity for independence, and induce us or obligate us to become or to remain dependent, docile... slaves!

"Going back to the land" doesn't have to mean a return to technological ignorance, nor "de-growth," nor be uniquely driven by ecological idealism. "Going back to the land" is, first and foremost, a return to independence.

Those who control food control the world, and those who control the world control you.[92]

Hygiene and Health

Our modern medicine is fantastic! Without a doubt, it has a major impact on our life: scanners, surgery, anesthesia, organ transplants, dentistry, eye surgery... The level of comfort and the list of services offered by modern medicine is impressive.

Nevertheless, this ultramodern and ever-more-perfect medical machine is also ultra-fragile. As in hurricane Katrina in New Orleans in 2005, the Haiti earthquake in 2011, a pandemic such as the Spanish flu pandemic in 1918, the nuclear accident at Chernobyl in 1985 and again at Fukushima in 2011, or an industrial accident such as Bhopal in 1984, health care services are always on the front line. They quickly lose control over the situation. In times of crisis we should expect rapid, potentially permanent disappearance of health care services, either because the hospitals lie in ruins, or because they stop

92 This is a paraphrase of a famous quote by Henry Kissinger: "Whoever controls food, controls peoples; whoever controls energy, controls countries; whoever controls money controls the world."

accepting patients due to lack of hospital beds, staff, medicines or ability to function autonomously...

How can an intensive care unit function without electricity? How can you prescribe pain control medications if they are delivered from across the world and are distributed on a daily basis, making their availability entirely dependent on the smooth functioning of the distribution system? How can doctors diagnose serious illnesses without access to special equipment and computers? How can a hospital function when it is deprived of electricity, running water, food, personnel or the ability to collect and dispose of medical waste?

Imagine for a moment the helpless situation in which you will end up if you have no medication, if you lose access to hospitals and doctors, even in case of a relatively trivial medical problem, such as appendicitis, a bone fracture, a deep cut, an infection, a fever or a severe toothache...

In any sort of catastrophic situation, in any part of the world, it is a major advantage to be in good physical shape.[93]

In addition, maintaining sanitary conditions allows you to prevent the development of medical problems and to continue to live in good health. In a difficult situation, the simple fact of having access to soap and clean water takes on a completely different meaning, because this allows us to maintain a high level of hygiene.

If a medical problem develops, you must be able to treat it effectively. The priority should be given to the statistically most widespread problems, but you must also foresee more

---

93 One must prepare for this in advance: to exercise, to eat right, not to allow problems to become chronic, not to become dependent on drugs, tobacco, alcohol, etc.

rare and complex ones. No doubt, you already have some things—what every mother has with her—such as a first aid kit with drugs for headache, bandages, antibiotics and antiseptics... The contents of such a first aid kit are easy to improve and enlarge in order to have the ability to handle booboos of a different sort and, in case of need, to help your neighbors and all those in need of your help.

It is very easy to sign up for courses in providing first aid, to learn the sequence of basic operations in case of an accident or a wound: to calm down, to look over the victim, to call for help, to take action, to reassure. We are not talking about earning a diploma or a certificate, but about learning basic medical principles and skills. For example, it would be useful for you to learn the following important skills: how to stop a hemorrhage; how to move a victim's body into a safe horizontal or semi-seated position; how to administer a cardiac massage, to disinfect and dress a wound, to treat a burn, to fix a dislocated joint, to make a splint for a broken bone...

Once again, we are talking about our independence from the system, about not running away from the problem but contributing to a solution.

Energy

Our everyday habits depend on abundant and cheap sources of energy. Their uninterrupted supply is only possible if the entire system functions perfectly. If it falters or collapses, we would be forced to say good-bye to keeping our bedrooms warm in the winter and cool in the summer, to running hot water on demand, to cooked food, to illumination that allows us to read in the evenings, to preserving food through refrigeration, to motorized transportation...

And what if all of this luxury were to disappear suddenly?

Of course, it would be a mistake to think that we would be able to maintain an optimal level of comfort: the ideal temperature between 19 and 26 degrees Celsius,[94] limitless electricity available at any moment, free access to gasoline and diesel fuel for our cars and so on. But we can maintain a minimal reserve, just in case: clothing and shoes, kerosene lamps, matches, batteries, the means for keeping warm and for running the most essential equipment...

In any case, it seems logical that if you reduce your needs and consumption, and at the same time create an effective traditional configuration for heating the dwelling and for generating electricity, you would then be in a position to achieve a more cost-effective and durable long-term result. And quite possibly, thanks not just to new technologies associated with renewable energy sources (solar batteries, rocket stoves and so on) but also thanks to older technologies from centuries past which will come back to us (Swedish stoves, kerosene lamps...) you will succeed in achieving full autonomy.

Knowledge and skills

Ownership does not imply ability.

Autonomy also implies acquiring the knowledge and the skills in vitally important, fundamental areas, such as first aid, preserving food (canning, vacuum packing, salting, pickling, smoking, fermentation, etc.), making and repairing tools and

---

94 66 and 79 degrees Fahrenheit.

furniture, agriculture, polyculture,[95] permaculture, hunting, fishing, animal husbandry and so on.

In a word, it is the opposite of specialization, and it's worth a lot!

How many different types of knowledge can we name? There are "hard" ones such as building a fire, making shelter, moving from place to place; there are the "soft" ones, such as telling a story, listening to one, learning something new, being curious, holding discussions; there are "technical" ones, such as everything connected with computers, mechanics, physics and so on.

We should note that the main goal of the educational system is, more and more often, to impart narrowly specialized, highly intellectual types of knowledge which cannot be implemented without an entire armory of technological and communications instruments, or outside of an ultramodern world that is functioning like a well-oiled mechanism. In essence, modern education, which is at the forefront of globalization and conformism, is creating entire generations of people who are physically incapable of taking care of their own needs and, in consequence, are entirely dependent on the system. Consequently, it has already become fashionable and traditional to denigrate traditional, manual skills and trades.

Defense

Whether we speak of maintaining our own physical or psychological integrity, or about defending others who are dear to

---

95 Polyculture is the opposite of monoculture. It is a method of farming where each piece of land is used to grow several plant species, thus creating a natural ecosystem—Editor's note.

us, or about defending property, the knowledge and the power needed to intelligently construct our defense must become an integral part of our strategy for achieving autonomy.

Let's recall Maslow's pyramid, in which the need for security is clearly defined and placed directly below our physiological needs.

Our interest in our personal security, physical inviolability, in our own well-being and that of those who are close to us is by no means reflective of any psychological disorder! Quite to the contrary, it is most natural... This is one of our inalienable rights and one of our main responsibilities. It is all the more important because, in spite of a few decades of relative tranquility in the more prosperous countries, we are once again confronting the realities of a predatory world. As Lenin wrote, "There is no abstract truth, truth is always specific" reminding us of the fact that a political lie is always disproven by the reality of the situation.

The specific reality is that our world does not resemble either the world we wish for, nor the world we recreate among our friends over a bottle of Merlot. Ideally, we would not have to concern ourselves with our personal security or about weapons... about defending ourselves or our children. Ideally, we would be subject to a completely different natural law, according to which our skin would be capable of photosynthesis, so that we wouldn't feel the need to eat other living things, and then no child would ever go hungry... Also, in that world there would be no evil people, no corrupt governments, no wars, no genocide, no violence, no hatred, no money, no shortages, no slavery, no murder... Oh, what a nice world that would be...

But our world is not like that.

Our world is, more often than not, cruel, violent and destructive, because it is to this day ruled by archaic and atavistic natural laws. With his ape-skin, man is not yet capable of photosynthesis.

This means that we have to act in accordance with reality. And in this reality we have to learn how to defend ourselves!

This is a very wide field for activity: mental preparation, self-defense training, martial arts, weapons training... The main question is, What must we know in order to be ready to defend ourselves and those close to us, to preserve our chosen and non-negotiable material, moral and spiritual way of life? Every person will find their own answer, loaded with meaning and with potential consequences.

The Social Bond

For millions of years our species lived not as isolated individuals but as tribes. We are social animals, and we feel the need to be members of large families, groups and clans. These social bonds were the primordial condition not for just our individual survival, but for the survival and evolution of our species.

From the point of view of anthropology, this stems from the fact that, on the one hand, our behavior is egotistical, while on the other hand we understand that we need others in order to survive, and are capable of altruistic behavior which a priori contradicts our personal interests. Freely performing noble and heroic acts, we underscore our merits and express our desire to unite with others—those we want to and can trust.

Traditionally such trust could be created, won or acquired only with the help of the surrounding social environment, family structure, which almost everywhere in the world is well disposed toward those seek unity with the group, follows its written and unwritten laws, and punishes unfaithfulness toward the group and unacceptable behavior.

Clannish behavior is still a feature of certain religions, criminal groups (mafia, gangsters and so on) and certain island and traditional cultures, but has practically disappeared in the contemporary world. It has been killed off by the urban environment, where anonymity predominates and where there are fewer social pressures to conform to rules and moral dictates, whatever they may happen to be. Moreover, our caring governments have done everything they could to make it so that, no matter what the problem, there would be no need for us to appeal for help to our family members or neighbors. The government is always nearby in order to help us, care for us, feed us, finance us, defend and support us. In fact, it tolerates forms of behavior which no clan would ever tolerate and would punish severely: laziness, asocial vices, self-destructive vices, crimes against other clan members, etc.

You can speak of belonging to a clan only when your behavior is defined by the following four interconnected elements:

Devotion: the tendency to identify with the clan members, with their reactions to and opinions of your aspirations.

Responsibility: the recognition of the fact that you are bound by previous commitments, and the feeling that you must give your time and energy to your clan.

Belonging: the connection of the clan to you, which must just as strong as your connection to the clan. As the Three

Musketeers put it, "All for one and one for all."

Faith: your faith in the positive value of the accepted norms which are necessary for the survival and well-being of the clan.

Mutual aid and solidarity have every right to become the plan and the strategy for achieving autonomy.

Starting today, you should work to develop faithful friends, support and encourage local small businesses, visit local farmers, talk to your neighbors and involve those around you with your projects!

Women and Autonomy

Our progression toward autonomy depends on our priorities, our family situations, health, financial resources and the environment in which we live.

We have seen how various crises—personal, local, regional, national or global—can cause fear and anxiety. And you, as women (as well as men), need to learn to make use of these feelings in order to think through, and then to motivate your actions directed toward achieving autonomy. These actions must be positive for your well-being and your future, as well for the well-being and the future of your children and of all those who are dear to you.

Instead of expecting help from a caring government or bureaucratic administration, even if it is sincere in its benevolent intentions, you as a woman—at first alone and on your own, and then, if possible, as part of a group—must develop your autonomy, learning to bear responsibility and to define your own life for yourself.

For a woman, as for a man, this means to strive for maximum independence of income (independent labor, entrepreneurship, constant learning that allows you to widen your horizons and always be aware of the latest), for maximum independence in nutrition (kitchen garden, treating yourself), for sincere and mutual relationships with family, friends, neighbors and society (at the scale of a house, a city blog, a village, a religious[96] congregation, or local associations), in order to be able to "sustain the blow" in case of financial or economic difficulties, security problems or more serious catastrophes...

The steps toward achieving autonomy need to be taken not just for the sake of buying a bit of insurance in case of a possible catastrophe or to avert some sort of collapse, but in order to foster healthy and well-founded resilience.

The intention to achieve autonomy is a lot more than a simple, instinctive response to crises. It becomes a well thought-out and conscious action, which allows us to create with our hands, first for ourselves, and then for others as well, a universe that to a greater or lesser extent will not depend on complex and unstable mechanisms.

This is a philosophy of life.

Is it possible to fulfill it? Who is doing it today? How can we find out more?

Let us start with something relatively simple. Numerous guides and internet resources (forums, blogs) provide us with a lot of high-quality information, but it is not always so easy to continue to act, because society is constantly urging us to do

---

96 The word "religion" comes from the Latin verb *religare*, which means "to reconnect."

the exact opposite. When it comes to women who have already started on the path toward autonomy, there are millions of them in the United States and thousands in France.

Rather than to speak in their name, I thought it preferable to give them the word.

In the second part of this book you can read the testimonies of women who have made a choice in favor of autonomy. Each of them is unique, each is different, with her own experience, her own worldview, her own profession, age and philosophical position, but all of them have been very interesting get to know.

Ladies, you have the word...

Part II. Women Talk to Women

"There are moments in Life when keeping silent becomes a fault, and speaking an obligation. A civic duty, a moral challenge, a categorical imperative from which we cannot escape."
—Oriana Fallaci, Italian writer (1930-2006)

Alina

> "Looking at the tins, I cried from happiness."

I am French. Every day my husband watches YouTube and reads Vol West.[97] When he sees a new post, he is as happy as a little child on Christmas eve.

He considers himself a squirrel that is squirreling away supplies for the winter, when everything will disappear. He is stockpiling food, water, medications, tools, gasoline, cash, seeds, books and so on.

Neither I, nor our family, nor our acquaintances knew anything of this, because he kept his supplies secret and stored them in his workshop, which is located next to our house.

Here is how I learned of his activities.

Some time ago, in the evening, he developed such a bad headache that he passed out. I immediately called the paramedics. They arrived quickly, but my husband only came to 36 hours later, in the hospital, in the intensive care unit of the neurology department.

The doctor explained to me that my husband had suffered a brain hemorrhage, and that he was lucky that I had called the paramedics right away.

All of this happened because of a blood clot which formed in the left hemisphere of his brain. My husband went blind in one eye, and the doctor couldn't say whether he would get better. He simply told me that my husband will remain in the

---

97 The first French language blog devoted to survivalism: lesurvivaliste.blogspot.com.

hospital no fewer than six months, during which he will undergo various analyses.

This was terrible news, because I had stopped working several years ago in order to have time to bring up our three children; the youngest had just turned four months.

Just as I had feared, after two months our bank account was almost empty, because France's social services only paid us 45 percent of my husband's salary. This money was enough to pay rent, electricity, car loan, insurance, internet and telephone.

That is, after all the fixed costs were paid there was nothing left. After two months we were high and dry.

I must admit, I cried a lot. But on that day I was forced to tell my husband that I had to kite a check in order to buy children's formula, that we have no more money for gasoline, and that because of this I won't be able to come together with the children to visit him next weekend—and I almost choked with tears. I hadn't told my husband anything about our financial situation before then, in order not to worry him, but this time I was forced to.

And then my husband informed me of the massive stockpile in his workshop. Together with the tins of food, he told me, I would find jerrycans of gasoline, cans of children's formula and 2,000 euro in cash in a coffee can.

I didn't know what to say. I didn't even know whether I should believe him... But it turned out to be the truth. Everything was stored in his workshop! When I saw these supplies, I felt as if I found a treasure trove. For the first time in my life I burst into tears from joy, looking at these tin cans!

I started to smile again. And I could go to visit my husband during the next weekend!

Ever since my husband left the hospital, I have been maintaining the stockpile together with him. Gradually we are rebuilding our little treasure trove.

For us the chore of maintaining the stockpile means more than just preparing for the worst possible catastrophe. It allows us to achieve a certain level of autonomy. In our case the catastrophe was brought on not by a hurricane, not by civil war, but a small blood clot a few micrometers in diameter.

Adriana

"It is possible to advance quite swiftly,
and with minimal resources."

I am shocked! How can you ask a lady her age... Mid-thirties, married, two children, seven and two.

Ever since childhood my pockets have always been full of all kinds of things. My grandmother and grandfather survived the war and formed in me the habit of keeping a small stockpile, just in case. I don't like to be taken by surprise. But don't they say that a woman's purse is an intuitive EDC Kit?

Ever since I got my own roof over my head, I am constantly evaluating potential risks: electricity outage, lack of telephone service, getting stuck in my car... I watch the development of French society and the crisis which the country is going through, because I know that sooner or later the modern system will suffer a crash.

A year ago a friend of mine gave me a book, signed by the author,[98] titled *Survive the Economic Collapse*, and showed me a few internet sites. That's how I found out that I am a survivalist. But the most curious thing is that my friend became a survivalist after he saw my stockpile. That's when he got to thinking!

The difference between me before and after that event is this: I gained a few good friends and I found out a lot about various internet sites devoted to the problem of survival... In this way, I became acquainted with the experiences—good or bad—of others. But most importantly, I rationalized and bal-

---

98 Piero San Giorgio.

anced out my preparations. For example, before I was quite far off-target in assessing the need for stockpiling drinking water...

I am not afraid that I will lose electricity, water, heat, because I've already experimented with these things. On the other hand, I am afraid of being robbed or assaulted, or of a pedophile attacking my children. I am also apprehensive that the current economic crisis will grow worse, causing unrest in the city, especially in light of religious hostility.

For me, preparations are a part of my everyday worries. Everything I do, ever moment, has to correspond to two concepts; namely, autonomy and the ability to survive. I am stunned by the high level of preparation of certain "preppers," Americans especially, who are much closer to these cultural conceptions than the Europeans. Some preppers have even been able to achieve a wide scope of autonomy in electricity generation, water and food... And all of this on the basis of an ECK. But that's not my case. But in the final analysis nobody is ever completely prepared. It's just that some are better-prepared than others...

When I lost my job (thank God, that particular crisis is already over!) I found myself with a lot of free time. But I don't have enough resources to achieve the ideal in terms of preparation. Today I am better-prepared than a year ago... but not as well as I will be next year!

I judge my needs in order of their importance and spread out the purchases in time. The minimal kit for survival, which every family must have, is the kit recommended by the government (a three-day supply of food and water, blankets, a portable radio, batteries). This kit is easy to purchase. It is affordable on any family budget, and this proves that money isn't everything. Free time allows me to gain new knowledge and experience. For example, I joined the Federation of French Marksmen.[99]

I would like to be self-sufficient in water and energy, but this is difficult to achieve. In my situation, it is currently impossible. Right now I am doing kitchen-gardening, which is quite effective. I hope that this once again becomes popular. Last year I was still a newbie, but now my activity has become more goal-directed. I try to optimize my planting, seed retention and harvesting. I am also learning to treat non-life-threatening illnesses using essential oils. Obviously, I got a certificate from taking a course on the basics of life safety. I must admit that the years when I belonged to a scout organization benefited me. I try to gain experience in many diverse areas: electricity, sanitary equipment, construction, and also food preservation, getting acquainted with the local flora and fauna, making household goods... This is a wide field for activity! I am never bored!

My relationship with my husband is very simple: I am in charge of everything! My husband lives within the cycle of "subway-work-bed," and devotes himself to our children when he has free time, usually on weekends. But I am the one who takes care of rotating our food stockpile and watches the money. As far as money is concerned, clearly, the more money there is, the faster the preparations can proceed. But it is important to understand that you can do quite well without numerous gadgets, that it is possible to find quality goods that are much cheaper than the famous, fashionable brands. And

99 See www.fftir.org.

since your neighbors will never find out how much you paid for your water filters, even though for some that's a drop in their ocean-sized budget, for others the savings can be quite meaningful.

In the final analysis there have been no cardinal changes, in the sense that we didn't just drop everything in order to buy an ECK in a rural place. But it is possible to find work anywhere, even though we are more of a family of intellectuals than farmers or manual laborers. Our values haven't changed either. They were always connected with the concepts of autonomy, stability... The most difficult thing of all is what's around us. The world cannot remain the same. In many areas there is already a decline. Now they are mending the holes, but this is slowing down a process that to us seems inevitable. Which generation will suffer the blow? Ours? Our children's? Our grandchildren's?

When it comes to autonomy, I see five main reefs for us to sail around:

Convincing yourself that it's all too complicated, that you can never prepare well enough, that nothing will happen, that a wonderful solution will appear at the last possible moment, that this only happens to others, not to you or those close to you... Consequently, you don't do a thing! That's a huge mistake!

Convincing yourself that in any case you will never be ready in time. But to be even somewhat prepared is much better than to not be prepared at all!

Falling under the influence of survivalist marketing and buying all sorts of random stuff.

Spending time in front of the computer and improving your theoretical preparation but doing nothing to move forward in practical, rational terms.

Thinking that you are better than others and will be able to handle everything on your own.

My close relatives know of the steps I am taking. To my great surprise, my parents are also working on improving their autonomy. My best friend is taking part in the survivalist movement. My husband thinks that this gives me something to do. And since everything that I do or buy turns out to be useful, he doesn't see anything wrong with it. Just in case, he says, we'll be prepared if something happens. That's not such a bad position to be in!

When it comes to my women-friends, here my results differ. When I reach out to them, hinting at the problems with the modern world, they usually don't respond. I try to recruit neighbors to my cause, but also in vain. They probably decided that I am a fantasist; meanwhile, they won't even last 72 hours! Few people know what items go into the minimal survival kit defined by our government. In debates, I always use the list prepared by the Ministry of Internal Affairs as an argument, since it's an "official" list.

When it comes to my children, I didn't alter their habits, because they are still small. I gradually acquaint them with the dangers of everyday life, teach the younger one to be attentive, so that he wouldn't get into an accident. The older one I teach to be vigilant and avoid contact with people who may turn out to be bad. When the children get older, I will try to pass on to them useful knowledge and experience, which these days isn't taught. The previous generations have lost a lot of knowledge, and have lost the ability to convey it, and we must try to correct this situation. I will try to do this unobtrusively. It will seem like we are playing a game. But most importantly, I will make sure that they will learn to see everything with a critical eye, that they will be able to see through the surrounding stupefaction!

I think that there is no fundamental difference between preparations for men and women. If people are conscious of the situation and the risks, they use similar methods. The difference comes from the fact that "men are from Mars and women are from Venus."[100]

I would like to explain to your women-readers that it is possible to move forward very quickly, even when your resources are insignificant. Then I would like to explain to them that there are a few different "schools of thought," and that they should themselves determine in what direction they should take steps toward independence.

And here is the message I would like to give to men. In survivalist networks I have met too many macho men, too few women and even fewer people who interpret this problem from the point of view of a family. And so, men, stop thinking of your wives as "little women." We know how to take care of ourselves! And with your help we will reach our goals!

---

100 An allusion to the identically titled book by John Gray.

Patriot Nurse

"Lead a measured life."

I am known under my nickname—Patriot Nurse. I am a registered nurse with a university degree. I grew up in a setting in which everyone foresaw everything and prepared for everything. In my family, they taught us from a young age to hold several solutions in reserve, and to behave flexibly in all situations.

My approach to preparing is based on rational calculations. Too many people who prepare think only about food and security, but underestimate the importance of medical preparation. But this kind of preparation for hard times is very important. I considered it my duty to tell people about this on my blog[101] and in my YouTube videos.

In my opinion the most probable risks for most people, and for me, are natural cataclysms, as well as financial, economic and currency crises.

But I am not afraid, because I have managed to prepare. Life is too short to be stressed out all the time. I found the time to lead a measured life and to treasure the beauty that appears before my eyes. Family and friends are very important to me.

When it comes to my priorities in preparing, let me say this: for me, a nurse, they are obvious. Aren't they?

In addition, I am maintaining a year's supply of food which I renew regularly. I also train physically, to be able to defend myself in case of aggression, and engage in sports.

---

101 See thepatriotnurse.com.

Let me repeat: I grew up in such an atmosphere that this is normal for me. There was no need for me to change my lifestyle. The only thing that bothers me is the cavalier behavior of airport security people. I am also afraid that my firearms will be stolen from my checked baggage (here, in the US, I have a license to carry).

I pay no attention to strangers. But if they show curiosity or take an interest in my preparatory activities, I calmly explain to them what I am doing. It doesn't bother me if they don't approve of it or find it funny. The only thing I can recommend to women who are trying to start preparing is to use their whole mind. Make your choices and live a measured life. It may turn out that the people around you will think that your actions are stupid or driven by your fears. In my opinion, the best response to that will be your calm, unhurried, sufficient and well thought-out preparation, which you can then explain and advocate. Preparing under the influence of fear may cause you to make incorrect decisions. But if you are going to prepare having thought everything out in detail, you will achieve excellent results.

And what can I say to men? Stand up for yourselves and be real men: strong, brave, polite, rugged! In the future, we will need reliable guides. And you can create that future with your actions in the present. We need you!

Jessie

"Decisive, capable, strong, rugged women—they exist!"

I am 30 years old, married, and I have two children, six and seven years old. I have equestrian and agricultural training, but I no longer work. Now I spend all of my time doing manual labor on our small farm with the goal of achieving food and energy autonomy. My husband is in the military.

In 2007-8, while doing research on the internet, I found out about the real condition of our system. I knew that it was dependent on fossil fuel energy, but I had not yet realized the high risks connected with future resource depletion. I decided to learn all about this subject. And then I learned about the state of natural resources, about the peak in oil production and about its economic consequences in a system where everything depends on growth. The charts instantly overturned all of my conceptions, in particular, about world demographics, which march in lock step with energy availability, rampant urbanization and the high vulnerability of civilization. The more complex a civilization—and this one certainly is complex!—the more vulnerable it is. It can disappear suddenly.

I had two small children. We lived in a country house, and my husband was moved to another job. We needed to plan our future. It was absolutely clear to me that we had to have a plot of land and to live far away from major population centers, nuclear power plants, dangerous industrial installations and so on.

We were young property owners, but in debt, because we bought the house during a period of high real estate prices, and were entering a period of mortgage crisis caused by the issuance of subprime loans. Our house had lost its value and it was difficult for us to get on our feet. We didn't want to keep it. We were forced to sell it, to find a new place to live that was more reliable for our security in the future, which we saw as quite challenging. And so, in a year we sold the house at a loss and started to look for a plot of land where we could establish our Sustainable Autonomous Base (SAB).

The main risk of which I was aware, and which really made me fear for the future, was a crash of the system in connection with Peak Oil. Only later did I start thinking about other, much more mundane risks. The first risk of which I thought was connected with hurricanes. We had already lived through several hurricanes. There is no electricity for several days, sometimes even weeks. This means closed shops, blocked roads, and a need to find a way out of this situation regardless of the circumstances. One must also remember about the risk of fires, nuclear and industrial accidents—in a word, about all the things for which we must prepare, at a minimum. In the end, it's a matter of common sense!

Every day I take steps which give meaning to my life. These steps are important for me, and they have become a way of thinking, a way of life, which suits my inner self. Can there be anything more normal than storing up supplies for the winter? This something people have done for ages. Is there anything more natural than knowing how to defend yourself, how to avoid becoming a victim, to preserve your physical inviolability? What can be more normal than maintaining good relations with the neighbors and knowing that you can always count on their help in case of trouble?

And so we are living on my husband's salary. This choice suits us very well. I have time to prepare, within the scope of our small farm, and my husband's income allows us to preserve our current lifestyle, investing in the long-term and in useful property. My motivation never weakens, because I am constantly reminded of what's happening by the news and the reality of the world.

Our main priority is an independent source of water. We collect rainwater, filter it, then pour it into a reservoir, to use for raising poultry and sometimes for irrigation. We also have a spring not far from our house. Producing food comes second. We have planted fruit trees, set up a kitchen garden, built a henhouse, bought a cow and we are trying to grow grains. We have some food in storage. But, to be honest, we are still far from being completely autonomous. Food autonomy is experimental work. It takes three years to learn to grow, breed and regenerate productive resources. Then we have to learn to produce them in sufficient quantities without any expenditure. I place a special emphasis on defense. It is very important for me. I am a woman, but by no means do I want to feel weak. I have never allowed anyone to bully me, and I don't want to be a victim. I want to have the ability to defend myself. The most aggressive and justified method is, obviously, through the use of weapons. I have learned to shoot and I am teaching my children to handle firearms. Now my family practices shooting, but purely for sport.

Almost all of our neighbors are hunters, and this means that they are armed. Nobody is shocked by this here. Aside from armed defense, to which, I hope, we won't have to resort, there is also defense without the use of weapons. I have learned several techniques of hand-to-hand combat which will allow me to avoid becoming a victim of aggression. But I understand that there is still a lot for me to learn, because such techniques will probably be the most useful in the future. My children are learning martial arts techniques and self-defense, in order to not be afraid of aggression and attacks. The most important thing for me is to teach them to deal with all situations with honor. They know several species of wild medicinal plants, they work together with me in the kitchen garden and the orchard, they catch mice...

Our supplies will last three to six months. I constantly renew them, because I do a lot of canning at home. I don't wait for the catastrophe to strike. I simply try to foresee everything. In this way, for me it is a cycle that is constantly being renewed. Every month we make small investments, buying hand tools. Obviously, the biggest investment was the purchase of the farm. We still spend most of our income on it, gradually improving it to the extent of our abilities. We spend very little on entertainment, because we are happy to be living in a rural setting. The most important thing for us is our project of achieving autonomy.

When it comes to distributing tasks, my husband hates housework. So what? I am perfectly capable of handling it by myself. Together we only do heavy labor. But stockpiling firewood and dealing with food production are my responsibilities. My husband is a wonderful and strict teacher of self-defense. We work toward each of us knowing how to do everything, so that we can substitute for each other if the need arises.

Some things have changed in my life: my husband and I became closer as a couple. My husband trusts me absolutely, as I do him. Every day I am doing something with my hands, and this gives me pleasure that few people get to experience. In the evenings I feel great, because of the surroundings and the physical labor, which is an inseparable part of our way of life. The most difficult thing is the feeling of alienation from society on an ideological level, to understand that so much is going wrong with it, and to feel powerless and limited.

I want to tell you a little story. My entry into the shooting club, which is basically a male preserve, did not pass unnoticed. A wonderful Dutch woman told me: "It will take a year for you to be accepted." And that's how it was! At first they looked askance at me, especially since I had the audacity to come wearing a skirt rather than a sporting outfit. But with the exception of a few retrogrades everybody was friendly toward me.

I think I was honest with myself and I openly explained to friends and family why I put so much value on a certain level of independence. Of course, I was often considered a pessimist, constantly being reminded that I shouldn't lose hope, that I must believe in the future. I replied that you can't use hope to make a sandwich, and that the future is more a product of willpower than faith. It saddens me that they refuse to see the real state of affairs, and can't offer any substantive counterarguments. But I consider this to be the result of human weakness and irresponsibility that's been inculcated in us by society. I am responsible for myself and my family, and will never place this burden on the shoulders of others.

I hope that in a crisis situation we will be able to unite with our neighbors, because it is always easier to handle adversity together. If such unity proves to be impossible, we will preserve our faith in ourselves and will try as hard as we can.

We do a lot of things together with our children. But we never tell them about situations that might cause them anxiety or upset them. We simply teach them to rely on their own abilities, to think about the situation, to look for solutions—but without any panic. We have already carried out some training exercises. For example, we have camped out overnight in the forest during wintertime. We demonstrated to them that there is much that they are capable of, and that they should believe in themselves.

When it comes to differences between men and women, I don't believe that there is a certain gender-specific inclination to strive for independence. Quite the opposite, I feel that creating a family with children is conducive to taking measures to keep it safe in case of need. When you are alone, you may lack the motivation. But if you care about one or more people who are dear to you, you naturally feel the need to defend them. Of course, this is a matter of character, convictions and the ability to step outside the bounds of one habitual behavior.

My advice to women: you should get pleasure from what you do. Planning for the future is only interesting if you know how to value the present. Having provided for your security, you can find happiness and the ability to develop freely.

I sometime read clichés about women that are spread by you men. This is unfortunate, because you deprive us of many possibilities. Decisive, capable, strong, brave and, at the same time, feminine women do exist! Learn to value them, not denigrate them. And know that we love you, especially when you are standing up for us.

Isabelle and Sophie

> "We are speaking about deep respect,
> not just for women but for others."

Allow us to introduce ourselves.

Sophie, 42, a doctor-therapist, has three adopted children (from Mexico), was married for 17 years, now living in a gay marriage for close to thee years. My main activities: cooking, reading, watching movies, kitchen-gardening, mycology, Chinese acupuncture...

Isabelle, 49, former employee of various international companies, working as a psychotherapist for a year and a half now, living in a gay marriage for close to three years. My main activities: kitchen-gardening, permaculture, mycology, phytotherapy, aromatherapy, massage, reading...

We live in a rural setting and hope to eventually create our SAB here. We own a plot of land of 2,000 m2 [half an acre], a large hothouse, kitchen garden, chicken coop, a cellar for storing cans and supplies, wells, steel shutters, and a two-meter-high fence...

We have noticed that a great multitude of women are either partially or completely resistant to the very idea of preparing for hard times and crises. This is surprising, since a woman should have a stronger natural self-preservation instinct than men. However, among the people engaged in preparing, 80 percent are men! Why is that?

In our opinion, women are overly reliant on their husbands in their unwillingness to lighten problems that can occur in the future. It would be interesting to find out what percentage

is made up of single women or women that are living in a ho-
mosexual marriage out of all the women who are preparing.
After all, such women can only depend on themselves.

We also think that it would be a mistake to try to convince
someone of the correctness of survivalist theories by appeal-
ing to fear and the necessity of defending oneself. But ap-
proaching it "through the refrigerator" or through a "natural"
approach would provide a good stimulus for women to prepare. This is precisely the way in which we have already convinced one woman, and are now convincing a second... And so,
don't keep talking to them about your EDC (Every Day Carry),
BOB (Bug Out Bag), SAB, etc. Just tell them about the "nest,"
about defending their families, about food supplies, a financial
reserve, foresightedness, the garden, natural products, gleans
(obviously organic), teaching children by going on hikes, about
time savings (organization), about the joys of doing something
with your own hands, feeling useful and valuable... In short,
start with the refrigerator and reappraisal of values... And be
"green"!

Based on our experience as therapists, we can say that
women are always worrying about their family. Consequently,
the goal of protecting it can serve as a wonderful means for re-
moving this worry. Let's be precise: this is suitable for women
who have a minimum amount of intellectual independence
and ability to think; that is, to regard all that is happening crit-
ically.

We must say that many women do not have any real financial independence that would allow them to be independent in
their opinions. Very often they are forced to obey their life's
circumstances.

We believe that women who have children are more likely to recognize the necessity of security, and, consequently, of autonomy, at least in the area of nutrition. And, in general, women like to garden. To help them understand the benefits that they can acquire from this sort of activity is to help them think about the future.

Finally, women don't always believe in their own abilities. Here we see the concept of the married couple, based on mutual respect. It is very important to value the woman. Tell her that she can achieve something, and she will do it.

For us, the most important thing is to learn and to do something every day.

Here are the types of our current activity: chickens, quail, planting, grafting, gardening, planting wild trees, permaculture, seed storage, harvesting edible plants, drying, pickling, canning, brewing beer, distilling alcohol, essential oils, fishing, mycology, natural substances for washing and cleaning, therapeutic ointments (for improved circulation, dermatosis, rheumatism), handcrafts, bicycle repair, cremes and shampoos, phytotherapy, aromatherapy, cheeses, deep massage, acupuncture, simple surgery, growing mushrooms (so far just trying to).

Today we have: a well, a cistern for water, a chicken coop, an aviary, a grain drier, a wood stove, a cauldron for pickling, an electric dehydrator for mushrooms, fruits and vegetables, a manual grain mill, a meat grinder, outdoor lighting, photovoltaic cells, bicycles, bicycle trailers, clothing for survival (footwear, coats, etc.), lots of tools and instruments, a large library (for knowledge and for pleasure), a stockpile of food for half a year and for exchange, fishing tackle (including a canoe), a large supply of medications, heirloom seeds in significant quantities, a 22 LR-caliber rifle (but no cartridges!), bow and arrows, knives, emergency kits, EDC-kits, Bug-out vehicle,[102] a fortified wall two meters in height, steel shutters, cellar, outbuildings, electric generator, wooden shelters.

What is left for us to do: replace the roof on the big garage and to install a system of photovoltaic cells, arm ourselves properly, create additional stores of food and medications for six months, prepare medicinal plants and essential oils, buy gold and silver bars to defend our purchasing ability from inflation, create a stockpile of fuel (constantly rotated), do more canning and drying of foodstuffs, fortify the entryway (the old oak door is very heavy but slightly cracked), install a container for better water supply, increase the stores of food for animals (chickens, dogs, cats).

We are respected in our little town, where we have settled down well. And we know quite a few people who are interesting to us because of their knowledge and experience.

What prompted all of this activity was an unusual event. The thing is, Sophie's husband, after the marriage fell apart and a loud argument, set the medicine cabinet on fire and then fled into the forest. Since then he has been sought by the police! It was at that very moment that we felt the need for security. We changed the locks and installed locks on the outbuildings. Now we never leave the house unattended. In connection with the disappearance of Sophie's husband we encountered numerous rumors—after all, it's a small town!—sometimes quite malicious. We had to come to terms with this disappear-

---

102 A Bug-out Vehicle, or BOV. This can be a car, a bicycle or any other means of transportation.

ance. At the same time we started to live as a same-sex couple. We felt a sharp need to create our "nest."

We no longer had a man in the house on whom we could rely, and so we tried to get by on our own. Since Sophie always wanted to have three or four chickens, we bought a chicken coop. Isabelle, who previously had a hothouse, bought a new hothouse in order to be able to grow flowers. We put the kitchen garden in order and planted nursery plants. We were experienced mycologists, and we constantly increased our knowledge. Over time we started picking more and more mushrooms. But a problem arose with storing them. Then we bought an Excalibur® dehydrator that allowed us to solve this problem.

After we bought the dehydrator, we understood that there were many other things that we can do ourselves. Then we started watching YouTube videos in order to understand what else we can do. Internet searches led us to Vol West's blog. This was a real revelation. All night long we would eagerly listen to his words, at first skeptically, then with interest and, in the end, with alarm and worry. We quickly assembled an emergency kit, an EDC-kit. Then we started thinking about what we can do for our home. In the end, we came across the Sustainable Autonomous Base concept and found out about your books. Ever since then we are constantly thinking and building.

Our path to achieving autonomy is through everyday involvement in new activities. Of course, autonomy is not an obsession for us, but it defines all of our actions and thoughts.

We experienced great stress and during three-four months we worked until exhaustion. Now we are moving ahead at cruising speed, not too high but constant. Before, preparing was our main activity, and we had no time to carefully prioritize our needs. Only now have we defined our goals. We are full of energy because we like what we are doing.

As far as the budget, we distribute the expenditure in accordance with the needs of creating the SAB. We have also realized that we must save on food, being content with what we grow ourselves, and invest our savings in purchases in our SAB.

To find the various goods we need we use the internet a lot. We often pay for them in three installments. We put aside cash that we get for giving consultations, and then use it for large purchases. We started making ointments for treating skin diseases and rheumatism. This brings us gratitude and a small income (purely symbolic). We have a lot of other ideas which will allow us to save a bit of money.

We have separation of labor. It arose spontaneously. Sophie is engaged in maintaining the stockpile and rotating stock, the kitchen garden, construction (wooden shelters, chicken coop). Isabelle controls the money, does canning, collects seeds and generates new ideas.

One of us is the "body": more elegant, but physically stronger. The other—the "head" (and a smoker). Every evening we discuss our patients, then talk about our plans. This happens perfectly naturally, while drinking a good bottle of wine. Susanne (she is 16) is the only one of the children who has decided to remain with us, and she is helping us with the household. We have a friend who is very handy. He does all the man's work around the house... and enjoys it.

Our way of life hasn't changed. What has changed, and quite radically, is our worldview. Now everything is focused on what we can find out and what can help us—what we can gather, do, build, save... Now we do our shopping differently and view others in a different light.

The most difficult thing is that we have to prepare by ourselves. But gradually those around us have started to embrace our ideas. After numerous explanations Sofie's parents have started putting together a small stockpile, and one of our patients has become interested in the project of autonomy. After all, due to the nature of our profession we really do inspire confidence.

Dangerous reefs await us primarily where fixed costs are concerned (we have to switch to photovoltaic cells as quickly as possible). It is also hard for us to put money into weapons, although we understand the great importance of this aspect of preparation. And so, weapons remain our weakest link. But we have secured our house as much as possible, although this is funny to say.

One way or another, our familial relationships have strengthened the bond between us.

We would recommend to the women who are reading this book that they store up water and food, learn to recognize edible plants and mushrooms and learn to use them, combining pleasure and usefulness, set aside a sum equal to at least the monthly salary in cash, convince their partner and their children to go along with the plan (for example, by letting them discover nature for themselves) and, most importantly, collect information, read, learn, experiment...

As far as men, as we see it, there are no differences in un-derstanding. There is perhaps a physical difference—and then hardly at all! With the help of men we would probably be able to meet our material needs more quickly (if they were very handy, of course). In a word, we are talking about fundamental respect not just toward women, but also toward men.

Veronica

"For my birthday I want an apple tree,
not a piece of jewelry."

I am 42, married, we have a six-year-old son, I give piano lessons (at home) and we have two dogs (a cocker-spaniel and a scotch-terrier). My husband is an engineer. He does shooting as a sport. We don't have any relatives living nearby. I am an orphan, and my husband is from the east of France. We live in a house on a one-hectare (2.5 acre) plot, overgrown with saplings, in a town of six thousand inhabitants, in the west of France. Last year my husband recommended that I read *Domino Theory* by Alex Scarrow. That was the moment when he became interested in survivalist theory.

I thought he went crazy, because he was stocking up on candles, ammunition for various kinds of weapons (he has been shooting at a sports club for six years now), water purification equipment and so on. Every evening he spent on survivalist forums, read books about preparing, worried about the future. He could only talk about the new information he acquired. This situation became tedious for me.

And then I told myself: I have to start paying attention to these forums and books in order to understand if perhaps he came under the spell of some sect or has become paranoid.

Then, reading your books, I understood that the world is turning strange, and that we really must gain independence, or things will be very bad for us. The point of departure became a desire to conduct an experiment which you discuss in your first book:[103] "Do you walk in the city? Do you feel safe?" Obviously, my answer was "No, no and no!" Even in our small town there are a lot of thefts, there are entire campgrounds inhabited by suspicious people, there are lots of cases of vandalism and so on...

What would we do in case of a hurricane, or if a financial crisis breaks out and rioters start disrupting things? I read your second book, co-authored with Vol West,[104] and also the book by Laurent Oberton.[105] You were right! We must prepare!

Luckily, we live in a geographic area with low climatic risks, if we don't count the storms, during which trees can fall. But we fear unrest in the suburbs, shortages of oil, financial crisis. Yes, I often think about these things. It has become my way of life. I am observing a constant increase in prices (electricity, supermarkets, medications and so on). This is another reason to plan ahead rather than suffer!

Luckily, this isn't stressful. Stress should not be allowed... Otherwise, how will we react if actual problems appear?

We prefer to "invest money" in food (I pay attention to promotions and discounts); clothes (I buy it at liquidation prices on the internet; my son even has a minimal set of clothes of all sizes through age 16); firewood—and not in a luxury car. Sometimes this turns into a game. It is a pleasure for me to optimize the locations of supplies in the house (I store cans according to date in the pantry, bottles of water are under the couch, extra clothing is stored in boxes under beds, the medical kit is always kept handy, and it never contains out-of-date

103 Pero San Giorgio, *Survive Economic Collapse*, Radix, USA, 2014.
104 Piero San Giorgio, Vol West, *Rues barbares—survivre en ville*, 2012.
105 Laurent Oberton, *France—Orange mécanique*, 2012.

drugs). We are well-prepared as far as heating and lighting (firewood for the fireplace, candles, kerosene lamps, warm clothes), nutrition, water and defense. My husband has firearms and he has taught me to use them. Watch out! During normal times we respect the law, but in case of extreme danger we will defend ourselves without hesitation!

I am planning to attend courses of the Red Cross for rescue workers, in order to learn how to administer first aid (I already have some knowledge of medicinal plants). I have planted a small kitchen garden, and I would like to get a few chickens. Finally, it is very important for me to maintain relations with the neighbors. I know that in case of a problem situation I have the means to feed my family and stay warm, at least for a few months.

Now when I read books I make notes and visit various forums. I use my notes to add to our supplies (food, medications, clothes, faming equipment, textbooks, school supplies).

My husband is involved in everything in the area of defense, supplies and water purification. He pays attention to the condition of the kerosene lamps, portable communications equipment and so on. He is extremely handy. He built a shed for storing firewood and made a cellar for various supplies. We regularly take out cash from the bank account. I also "invest" in bottles of alcoholic beverages, in order to have the ability to barter them for other products in case of emergency.

It may seem strange, but this way of life has allowed me and my husband to become closer. We like to discuss our home—our SAB. There is nothing complicated, because the urge to achieve autonomy has become our way of life. For my birthday I dream of getting an apple tree, not jewelry!

In the next stage we want to get into shape, lose a few pounds, start leading an active life and increase our knowledge (defense, gardening and so on).

Our six-year-old son already knows a few self-defense moves. He knows that there are weapons in the house (in locked safes). A little later he will learn how to handle them and how to shoot, obeying all the safety rules and with us watching him. Next year he is going to start going to Tae Kwon Do classes. I am also teaching him the basics of gardening, medicine (disinfection, taking care of one's health), taking care of dogs. In principle, I try not to coddle him too much, and allow him freedom of action and the opportunity to find ways out of situations on his own (he already has a small children's Swiss Army knife). I teach him not to be afraid of life's situations and of meeting strange people, to learn to judge the level of danger (yes, you can use a self-defense move, but you have to use it correctly). We teach him that being someone is more important than how you look. It's a real philosophy of life.

Independence is very important for me, because it it is part of my character. Now I don't look for excuses, I have become more proactive and self-assured. I know how to express my thoughts, to argue for my ideas, to make others respect my choice. I am proud that I have stockpiles. Before I would make jokes about my mother-in-law when she was making stockpiles when she only had 50 euros left. Now I have become like her! I am happy to know that my husband can count on me. I have even been able to set aside a large sum of money, because I have learned to control our supplies. In addition, I never make purchases in a hurry. In case there is a problem I am able to stay calm.

Gradually my female friends have also started to build up stockpiles. But they are afraid of emergency situations, such as crises, unrest in the suburbs, hurricanes. Many of them are not accepting reality and are idealizing our "caring" government. The same applies to their husbands, who don't want to believe that a crisis can erupt in France. As far as my husband's parents, they live in a village. They have always been survivalists, without even suspecting it!

It is essential to change our mindset: not to expect help from a "caring" government, but to be open to the needs of survival. Do you have insurance? Well then, you should also have stockpiles! We need to look out for ourselves. Unfortunately, this is no longer part of the French mindset. We have turned into a country of people who receive help! And these people take pleasure in their mediocrity and only know how to complain, instead of taking care of themselves. Prove to me that I am mistaken!

My husband and I like your writing style very much. You provide the key for thought, you point out ways out of situations. But we must get out of difficulties ourselves. Thank you!

We think that it is necessary to stop moaning and to start acting.

Sylvie

"We have become a more close-knit
family."

I was born in 1975 in the Somme region. I am married with
three children: two boys, nine and six, and a girl of three. I am
a housewife, because I don't want my children to be brought
up by strangers. I want to be close to my children and get the
maximum pleasure from their presence. I like animals, nature,
I love autonomy and firearms. My husband, same as me, is a
lover of autonomy. We have common views and common pursuits.

I became interested in survivalism around five months ago.
Actually, deep down I always felt the draw of survivalism, but I
wasn't taking any practical steps. I used to like American disaster movies, such as *The Abyss*, *2012*, *The Road*... But now when I
watch such movies I think about my children, and these
thoughts change my perception of things in light of a crisis. I
started to seek out information on the internet. Since my husband hates his job, we started to look for a simple life with the
goal of minimizing our expenditures, to live on the money we
have, to escape from this consumer society...

In looking for information, I came across Vol West's web
site, and Piero San Giorgio's books.

I created a Facebook page in order to follow events and to
maintain a dialog, although before I never had any interest in
social networks. I "armed" myself with their books and those
of other authors, listened to several lectures by the journalist
Pierre Jovanovic, contrarian analyst Olivier Delamarche, politi-

147

cian François Asselineau, journalist Michel Collon... This became my point of departure in understanding the lies spread by mass media.[106]

For me, the most likely risks are constantly increasing unemployment, mass immigration and the constant lying of mass media. Moreover, I am observing the constant increase in the cost of food, which more and more often is turning into junk food. In a word, our society has become unstable and ready to explode at any moment. This will lead to economic collapse, and will end in civil war...

For half a year I have been waiting hopelessly for an interview at the employment center! "We have too many requests, we have no time, we will call you." Luckily, I wait for this interview not so that I can live. More and more companies are closing... Generally speaking, we are too dependent on the system. I understand that our society is sick, and that this disease is progressing with each passing day.

For me preparation is a task that occupies my every second. Over the past few months my family bought (at liquidation sales) a small tractor, a hand mill, a press, seeds (heirloom), an emergency kit, food, water. We have signed up for a course in firearms training. We prepare every day. For example, when shopping, I always pick up something extra (water, tins of paté). I have enough energy for all of this, because I know that our choices and our preparations are very important. The wider my outlook becomes, the more convinced I become that we must prepare without delay.

---

106 In his books Michel Collon uncovers the lies spread by so-called "official" sources of information in the mass media.

We have humble needs, and because of this we succeed in putting money aside for our preparations even from the salary of a small public official. I have a neighbor. He is a devout con-sumer, and it pains me to watch how he works all day long, and even makes some extra money in the evenings. And all of this just for the sake of buying a motorcycle, then a car, then another car. He says that he has to spend the money as soon as he earns it, otherwise he gets bored. I find this pitiable.

Here is what our preparations include:

Food: permaculture, canning, bread, yoghurt...

Safety: having a good medical cabinet with antibiotics, emergency kit.

Water supply: containers for collecting rainwater, filters

Energy independence: wind and solar energy, gas. I am al-ways looking for a better solution, because there are few sunny days where we live.

Defense for myself and my family (learning to shoot). I think that this is very important.

Taking money out of the bank: I take out the maximum amount, leaving just enough for paying utility bills. I also ex-cluded all unnecessary expenditures.

Basic knowledge and skills: household equipment and in-ventory, gardening... I want to become more capable of physi-cal labor and more inventive!

The most difficult thing: finding friends who are tuned into the same thing as me. I have tried to talk calmly, without rush-ing events, with my relatives, friends neighbors... But it is hopeless! When you are trying to explain a problem, people think that you are paranoid. And at this moment I have given up on further efforts. I am a little bit sad about them. I tell my-

self that for them the fall will be swift, because they are completely helpless. But I am glad that on Facebook I have met a
lot of people with whom I can share my thoughts, advice and,
finally, to feel that I am being understood.

Every month I take a small sum of money out of our savings
to buy two-three things that are missing. When I am shopping,
I buy a little more than needed, if I can afford it.

My husband is preparing by upgrading and maintaining the
house, the entire energy system, the kitchen garden, where we
practice permaculture. He likes to find out new things on the
internet.

I help him, keeping accounts and doing shopping. When my
husband needs to buy something, I see whether we can afford
it this month or if we have to wait a little bit.

My father is helping us. He likes to find old tools at liquidation sales: hand mills, presses, cast iron cooking utensils... In
truth, he thinks that we need these things for decorating the
house.

Since we started on preparation we have become a more
tight-knit family. We consume a lot less and we are proud that
we are not going down the path of conformism that our society forces upon us. Even the children like to help out, especially with taking care of the garden... I have explained to
them, unobtrusively, without causing anxiety, that it is very
important to be autonomous and to eat well. In spite of their
young age, they understand us. I explain to them why I do
things a certain way and not another, and why we are preparing. They help us out as much as they can, helping us with the
gardening. We teach them the basics of survivalism (how to
purify water, how to light a fire). They like helping out and

talking about this. We feel ourselves stronger, better-prepared than others, and this calms us down.

No matter what happens—a crisis, a flood, snowstorm, war —independence is first and foremost. This winter, because of a snowstorm, we were trapped for a week. That is not so long, but I was happy that we have food stockpiles. After that I quickly restored them.

The only regret I have is that I haven't been able to relocate to one of the central regions of France, where nature is richer and more diverse. But it is very difficult to sell the house. That is why we are preparing where we live. In any case, it's not so bad here, because we have settled on a big farm, where, in case of need, we can shelter our entire family. We have to know how to help those near to us. We have the advantage that we live far away from big cities, and our village only has 90 inhabitants.

To women who are reading this I recommend that they start by looking for useful information on the internet. It is possible that you will be struck by the same idea that struck me. And then you should try to make at least a small stockpile of food and water. Think about your current situation and way of life, leave the city, if that's a possibility, start to prepare for autonomy together with your husband or partner, if you can, because women think about important things that men tend to ignore, and vice versa.

In conclusion, I would like to say to the men that they should encourage their wives to take up martial arts and shooting, because in case of a serious, very serious crisis women, in the absence of men, must be able to depend only on their own abilities in order to defend themselves and their children.

Ingrid

"My friends consider me an extraterrestrial."

My name is Ingrid. I am 34 years old, unmarried, no children. I was educated as a geologist. On weekdays I am a web designer, and on weekends I am preoccupied with reconstructing the lives of the Vikings. For as long as I remember myself, I have always stood out in having foresight, and this is thanks to my grandmother who, having survived two wars, always told me how important it is to have in the house a supply of food, water, matches and candles that would last for several weeks. My passion for reconstruction and my many holidays, which I spend far away from everyone, have taught me not just to make stockpiles, but also to do many things with my own hands. But I have only started to really systematically structure my preparation in the middle of last year, after I have read the book *Survive the Economic Collapse*.

Obviously, thanks to my education, I already knew of such a concept as Peak Oil. I knew that the limited reserves of mineral resources, on which we depend, will in the end create serious problems for us. But I didn't realize how unavoidable this is until I read your book. I noticed the symptoms which foretold several types of crisis, but I didn't understand that these types can overlay each other. If you don't take into account personal risks (fire, flood) then, after some time, I believe that the economic risk will come first, accompanied by disturbances of ecological character. In short, reading this book coincided with the moment when I started wanting to return to a more austere, more autonomous life closer to nature. Everything got mixed together. The result was my current preparations, which are far from finished.

All of my free time, all of my leisure is spent on acquiring independence while preserving my personal responsibilities. Preparation relegated my hobby of many years to the background from the point of view of time, money and interest. Sometimes I feel stressed, because days seem too short to me. Time flies imperceptibly, and I often get the feeling that I am not succeeding in getting enough done.

In order to have the possibility of getting everything accomplished without collapsing from exhaustion (as it was in the beginning) I had to learn to carefully plan my activities, allocating certain time windows for solving this or that problem outside of work, to plan out each month and to distribute in time the purchases of food and other goods in order to stay within the monthly budget. I also had to limit the number of holidays devoted to reconstructing the lives of the Vikings, and the amount of money I spend on my hobby.

I was also forced to stop and to rest when necessary, in order to avoid becoming exhausted, to pay attention to the needs of my body to avoid going too far, trying to do everything at once, as in the beginning.

Obviously, my priorities in the process of achieving independence are autonomy and skills connected with satisfying my vital bodily needs: gathering, filtering and purifying water, cultivating the kitchen garden (while looking for a house I am simultaneously, more or less successfully, trying to grow certain plants in my apartment), breeding rabbits, fishing, hunting, canning and processing food. I also want to learn to make certain things (soap, toothpaste, candles), to sew clothing, to tan skins, to make ceramics. These skills are very important for me, because I don't want to have to keep particularly big stockpiles of manufactured items around me and depend on them. Also important for me are medicinal herbs and defense. Thanks to my unusual hobby, I have already acquired some skills (spinning, weaving, basket weaving, using plant-based pigments, sewing by hand, embroidery, gathering, sword fighting, archery) and this allows me to spend my time on other activities, which I haven't yet mastered.

As far as my supplies, I have sorted them out based on their expiration period. I use the principle of FIFO (first-in, first-out), gradually replacing products as I use them up. Because I live alone with a dog I have the ability to independently set my budget. In this way, all I had to do was reorient toward preparation the resources which I previously spent on my hobby. However, the fact that I live by myself limits me in terms of having a bigger, common budget, and, more importantly, requires extra work, because I don't have the ability to distribute responsibilities between two or several people in the course of preparation.

Preparing has forced me to completely rethink many everyday, exclusively female problems; for example, the period need for certain items of hygiene. To avoid having too big a stockpile of tampons and sanitary napkins, even reusable ones, I was forced to look for alternatives. My choice was to use a "mooncup"[107] (a barely advertised but very practical system). I

107 A "mooncup" or a menstrual cup is a small bell-shaped container with rounded edges, usually ending in a stem to make it easy to withdraw. It is usually made of medical silicon, and sometimes out of medi-

also started to change my daily diet to bring it in line with my future autonomy in food. This process has turned out to be quite difficult and is far from complete because I am too habituated to many products; for instance, to chocolate! I have joined a local shooting club, forcing myself to go there regularly and to plan my time. This fundamentally changed my schedule, forced me to organize my time differently and reshuffle my priorities as well as finances, and this is not always easy, especially considering that unforeseen expenses can pop up at any moment.

Thanks to my hobby, I am used to living humbly, without excesses, to working on a farm and to living using the old-fashioned ways. A simple life and the need to do things with my own hands does not create any special difficulties for me. But the financial aspect remains for me the main stumbling block, because I live alone, on a single, modest salary. This seriously impedes my progress toward independence (including

---

cal thermoplastic elastomer or latex, depending on the make, and can be either quite flexible or somewhat stiff depending on model. A woman inserts it into the vagina by hand and carries it inside during menstruation, allowing menstrual blood to gather inside it. Unlike a tampon or a napkin, the cup does not absorb blood and does not allow it to leave the body. During menstruation it is necessary to empty the cup two-three times a day and rinse it in drinking water. It is not recommended to hold it inside for more than 12 hours in a row without washing it. Between menstruations the cup should be sterilized in boiling water, then stored in a container, which is normally sold with it. Different types of cups can be found on the internet or in shops that sell natural, ecological or alternative products. A menstrual cup can be reused many times. The useful life indicated by the manufacturers can be as high as 10 years.

the fact that so far I can't afford to buy a house that isn't too far from my work).

As far as my friends, because of my unusual hobby they have always regarded me as strange. And so I haven't felt any-thing different. My colleagues and friends think that I am an extraterrestrial. And only a few people, who understand the situation and are also preparing, coordinate their actions with mine in order to unify efforts. The rest—and they are in the majority—are not sufficiently farsighted (women especially). They do not understand what I am doing and think it absurd. But I live well, because I have learned to pay no attention to the opinions of others a long time ago, especially if their only everyday care is looking for fashionable footwear, a new dress or some other accessory that they are planning to buy. The same thing goes for my family.

My nearest surroundings (what I call my "heart family") consists of people who understand the situation extremely well. These people do not look askance at me or my actions, do not pose questions about their social acceptability. Their opin-ions are especially valuable to me.

Living alone, having severed all connections with my bio-logical family, I care not just about my own defense, but about the defense of my "heart family." That is precisely why I try to include them as actively as possible in my process of prepara-tion and urge them to join efforts, to be able to defend each other. I have also convinced several members of my "heart family" who did not know how to defend themselves to take some self-defense courses, in order to have the ability to stand up for themselves in case of need and not to depend on the help of others.

I suspect that for me, as a woman, this striving for independence has a tremendous significance also because, in spite of the battles fought by the previous generations, I still meet a lot of women who place on their husbands and partners the burden of worrying about various aspects of life (for example, worrying about an income that can support the entire family, or about defending the family). Many women think that they should give men the opportunity to control everything and organize everything, because that's "man's work." Moreover, when talking about preppers and survivalists with uninformed people, in their imaginations there immediately arises the image of a young man, armed to the teeth, ready to shoot dead any poor person who might walk through their garden gate. In our collective subconscious preparing for various difficulties is also considered "man's work." I think that many women believe that this is none of their business because deep in their soul they are still convinced that there are typically female tasks, and that there are also typically male tasks, and that preparing and trying to become autonomous falls in the category of male tasks.

What advice can I give to women? Only what I have already offered to my women-friends with a varying degree of success: first gather information, watch internet videos and visit various web sites, buy the book I already mentioned and find really useful for newbies, don't shy away from using social networking to stay abreast of new developments and to understand which books you should buy and which to skip. But most importantly, I would advise them—if they haven't done this yet—to register for self-defense courses; for example, Ninjitsu,[108] Jiu-Jitsu,[109] Krav-Maga[110] or ROSS,[111] which will work where you live, and to learn to administer first aid and gain basic skills.

To the men who are reading these lines I want to say this: don't hesitate to involve your wife or partner in your preparations, and not just as an assistant, but as an equal partner on your path to independence. Urge her to discuss this subject with her women-friends, because I think that it is easier to convince women of the necessity of such steps if a women talks to them who is herself actively preparing. And then they will understand that this is not at all the sort of work that is designated specifically for men.

---

108 Japanese martial art.
109 Japanese martial art.
110 Israeli martial art.
111 Russian martial art (Russian national system of self-defense)

Valerie

"Difficulties are arising very close to us."

I am 39 years old. I am Belgian, married 20 years already, and I have two daughters, 19 and 16. I am a nannie, and every day up to five children younger than five gather at my house. I like everything having to do with nature (animals, walks, gardening, flowers), reading, meeting friends, family...

We have always kept all sorts of supplies at home. We are used to living this way. My husband is the sort of man who always tries to find out more, to make things better. He finds a lot of information on the internet. It was he who discovered this parallel universe, the world of survivalists... He talked to me about autonomy and independence, he gave me your books to read... Even before I knew of many things, but I did not realize that the hour has come... The time has come to deepen our knowledge, to perfect our skills and know-how, because the familiar world of well-meaning citizens is ready to blow up, to fly into pieces...

The greatest risk that I need to avert in the future has to do with passive and active defense of the house and its inhabitants. We live in a suburb of Brussels. Having read your Barbaric Streets,[112] and realizing that it is unlikely that I will be able to move to a different place, I allocated the topmost priority to defense, and also to obtaining knowledge in the area of medicine.

---

112 Piero San Giorgio, *Rues Barbares*.

We prepare every day. For example, instead of going on vacation somewhere far away (oh, how I miss the scents of Ardèche...) we economized and bought a small farm with one hectare of land with the intention of building a chicken coop there, starting a kitchen garden, planting an orchard, breeding rabbits... We spend all of our weekends and holidays on the farm, collecting fruits and vegetables, making preserves.

This is not at all stressful, because it is impossible to avoid reality. You have to get done as much as possible, using the resources you have, and given the time, the concrete moment, when you can get it done... The only thing that worries me is defense of our dwelling. Where we live there are neighborhoods that have a bad reputation, inhabited by people who have not integrated into our society, and there are large bands of underage criminals operating there.

My husband spends all of his time at home, and I also work at home. Because of this, we have the ability to do things gradually, during the day. We also have evenings and weekends at our disposal... We have lots of motivation and energy, but we do everything rationally, gradually (especially the hard physical work). Budget? Ohhh... Unfortunately, because of my work, this is a headache, because I don't have a steady, fixed salary. But it's better than nothing... Each cent is spent to achieve a goal, or to save and to make purchases later. Of course, our preparations are proceeding very slowly.

Here are our priorities: to increase our food stockpile (here we are well-defended, because we always buy more than we need and do canning at home). Defending the home also seems important to us. It gives us a feeling of satisfaction to look around us, but there is a lot that's still left to do... It would be good to achieve autonomy in the area of electricity, to not have to worry about the future budget... Water is no problem for us, because we have many cisterns. We need to stockpile a large amount of wood (we have two wood stoves on which we can cook). We need to buy everything that's necessary for the medical kit. We need to expand our library (in case we lose internet access). We need to take courses in self-defense.

The important skills are: gardening, in order to be self-sufficient; caring for animals, monitoring their health and their lifecycle; butchering animals by ourselves; tanning leather; learning to cook differently; get practical skills working with sanitation equipment and electricity and knowing how to repair it; learning to live without electricity and knowing what to replace it with; learning to sew and to mend clothing; learning to make things with our own hands; making it so that each member of our family and our clan is independent, in case one of us dies; learning to use weapons—this ability also seems important to me. Perhaps I forgot something... Learning to be ready for any situation that's different from the current norm...

Of course, we are always postponing new purchases and using up what we have already bought. We pay our bills first, and only then do we plan what is important to buy for ourselves and for the house. If in a certain month we can't afford anything, we wait patiently... If we have the ability to get certain things done on our own, that's what we do, instead of spending money... Our younger daughter is less active (without a doubt, due to her carefree youthfulness). My husband is in charge of everything that's outside the house. My elder daughter helps me with the animals. I do my work and everything else I can. But it is obvious that it is always possible to do more...

Our striving for independence hasn't changed much, because it was already at the base of our way of life. After realizing the state of society and understanding that we lack sufficient financial resources we chose to limit the number of times we go out and to cancel vacations. This was a hard choice. But we look forward to the future with hope and prefer to think that we have chosen correctly...

It is very hard when you lack financial resources. But you shouldn't allow yourself to feel powerless, you have to take control of yourself and do as much as you can, using the resources that you do have...

I am not the least bit concerned what strangers think of us. We already have plenty of interesting people to talk to, who give us constructive advice. In the worst case strangers think of us as alarmists. But I have to admit that what saddens me the most is the fact that, in spite of my advice, many of my friends are not prepared...

In order to have the ability to defend ourselves we have registered for firearms training courses and got licenses[113] for using weapons for sport. Of course, we handle firearms very carefully. Soon my daughters will also learn to use all the kinds of weapons that we have. In my opinion the best kind of defense comes from mutual help of neighbors.

It is very important, especially for a woman, to know how to defend yourself. In everyday life and, most importantly, in extreme situations you must not allow women to end up in positions of weakness. We, women, can become targets for mani-

___
113 See www.tir-sportif.be.

acs, sexual and otherwise. And so we must know how to stand up for ourselves, because any man—if we are alone—will be unprepared to discover that we are equipped with knowledge, skills and methods of self-defense. This will allow us to withstand attacks. It is very important to prepare not just physically but also spiritually.

Preparation can lead to a certain amount of tension over fewer restaurant meals and other pleasures. But it forces us to teach responsibility to our children, so that they would understand the situation and the reasons for our efforts, and the sacrifices we have to make as a result. Preparation leads to an interesting and constructive exchange of opinions. For example, our younger daughter reminded us that it is very important to stockpile alcohol and cigarettes, in order to be able to use them in barter... Our daughters are very excited about learning how to shoot. We are all open to dialogue and discussions. But the main thing that I want is for my daughters to understand that this is more than just a way of life, that this will become a survival instinct which they will pass on to their children, and which will not disappear when we are no longer alive.

I want to say to the women who are reading this that they should begin by appraising their surrounding situation. Is it a good place to live? Is it secure? Is it suitable for autonomy? After that everything will follow naturally: stockpiles, autonomy in electricity generation, heating, kitchen garden... Perhaps it would be better to just give you a good book on the subject and then discuss everything over a cup of coffee... In this way, it will be possible to formulate a plan, and a list of things to get done first!

As far as the husbands, I would like to say to them that it is not necessary for them to follow their own plan. They need to explain, to exchange information, to read articles together, to gather together with friends and hold discussions. This is good to do, and it's effective. Same thing applies to friends, fathers... Rely on your own experience, and explain that difficulties can arise right next to you and that many people are asking questions and expressing their doubts... Women are by their nature stable, and consequently all it takes is one step to understand and to join...

Nélia

"Leave me my sneakers!"

I am French of Algerian descent, 34, married, with no children. I am a lawyer working in Paris. My husband is a pharmacist. I was born in a family of Kabyl immigrants, in a suburb that has a bad reputation throughout France. I have five brothers and sisters, and survival was always a problem for my family because of our fear of the Apocalypse, and because of that we always had to somehow survive until the end of the month. We were constantly economizing on everything. Since my mother, as a real Mediterranean native, always stockpiled incredible quantities of semolina flour, sweet potato, couscous (my father always bought everything in 20 kg bags!) and since I was a very studious girl and got good grades, we had to keep away from vandals and thugs who were constantly ruining the lives of people in our neighborhood.

Five years ago, as part of my job, I read a lot of books about debt. That is how I found out the truth about the real state of our contemporary financial system. It is perfectly clear that it will collapse in an instant! My relatives in Algiers survived a period when the country partially collapsed. I am convinced that the same thing will soon happen not just in France, but in the United States and the United Kingdom... everywhere!

Since my husband and I live in the city and work until late, we decided to keep a minimal stockpile at home (candles, food, water and so on) and also to prepare a place where we could hide if it became necessary. My husband's parents (they are Tunisians) have a small house in the central part of Tunis. It is far away, but the house stands on a big plot of fertile land. And so we decided to spend some time there to put the house in order. We installed solar water heaters, replaced large but very old water cisterns, installed a wood stove—which is not a luxury because the house is very cold in the winter because of poor insulation.

We asked our neighbors to help us work the land when we are in France (it's mostly pasture but there is also a small kitchen garden and a henhouse). We will be able to shelter our relatives, but by no means all of them! For example (don't tell anyone!) I have a brother who does nothing. He just lives on government aid. It doesn't matter that we are related, he is too lazy, and we don't want to see him around!

What upsets us most of all is the political situation that has emerged in Tunis after the "bearded ones" arrived. But now there are plenty of "bearded ones" in France as well! Yes, we are Moslem, but we are not extremists. We don't drink alcohol, but I don't wear a hijab and I wish to preserve my freedoms, even if things go badly. Let me have my sneakers!

When we come to Tunis we work the land in order to achieve food autonomy. We have already started to stockpile cans in the cellar, olive oil, installed an electric generator, bought a supply of gasoline.

My husband and I decided that if things go badly we will open a small pharmacy in the village and will sell preparations based on wild medicinal plants. Since my husband is a pharmacist, he started studying ways to prepare medications from local plants. We already started to buy the equipment for drying, storing and combining medicinals.

We have come up with a way to quickly leave Paris in case serious problems arise. We both have open tickets to Tunis. If planes aren't flying, we plan to reach our friends in Marseilles,[114] and there board a ship. In an extreme case... there is still the path through Italy and the Strait of Sicily. We are still working out the details of this last plan!

My girlfriends and our friends think that we are crazy. But I respond to them that they also have food stockpiles "in case relatives come to visit"... I do not discuss this with colleagues, although in dinner conversations they too admit that it's all going very badly. But they never follow their train of thought to a conclusion!

Since we don't have any children yet I don't have to address the question of their upbringing. But if I had children I would want to give them a traditional upbringing, close to nature, without television, video games and the rest of what makes children stupid and dulls their minds. As far as religion, I consider it a personal decision which should not be discussed in public or forced upon children.

To women I would say that they should work together with their husbands and that such joint work is good for a couple's relationship. To be prepared means to be more independent. No matter what happens, all is *maktub*.[115]

And you men, don't pretend that you are macho, don't think that you know everything, and learn and help us to defend our families. Women need you as partners, not as bosses! (I don't mean my husband, because with him all of this is as it should be.)

---

114 A major French port on the Mediterranean.
115 Arabic for "it is written"; an expression that implies that everything that happens is fate.

Marie-Claire

"I am a sort of conductor."

I am 37 years old, married, with three children (three and a half, five and ten). I am a nurse, French. I worked in Paris for 10 years, then left for Morocco in order to create a clinic for heart surgery there together with my husband. In June of 2012 I stopped working professionally (had enough!). Now I am a housewife, but I am an activist in a citizens' movement.

I don't remember what served as the real reason for awakening in me an interest in survivalism. The process went on gradually, as I acquired life experience and became acquainted with the views of other people (my paternal grandmother experienced great difficulties in surviving World War II and often told me about them). The move to Morocco opened my eyes on many things; in particular, the disconnection between the lifestyles of different social strata, on the consumer society in the West, on the insufficient environmental defense in developing countries... People who have the opportunity to travel (but not the ones who live in hotels!) have a more realistic view of the world. I think that I first became interested in ecology. I read many books, and my interests spread to permaculture, and then to survivalism. Three years ago I became bedridden for three months because of a paralyzed right leg. This gave me time to think about myself, about my marriage, about our family!

In addition, I downshifted: I sorted out my own priorities.

Reading articles about Peak Oil, I understood the importance of the time factor and the seriousness of the situation.

168

Living in Morocco, we can encounter political problems, which is our main problem. Events can unfold quite swiftly. Consequently, we have to be prepared to flee the country at any time, or have to deal with social unrest. In spite of an economy that is developing relatively quickly, Morocco's government debt is quite high. This means that unpopular economic measures will be taken: a decrease in social payments or a devaluation of the dinar. In either case this will lead to increased prices for essential foodstuffs (sugar, tea, coffee, oil, flour and, in consequence, bread), for diesel fuel (right now it's 8.75 dinar/liter, which is 0.87 euro/liter) and natural gas (there are no gas mains here and everyone cooks with propane from tanks). This will be a catastrophe for the people, most of whom are surviving on incomes of between 2,000 and 4,000 dinars (or 200-400 euro; minimum wage comes to 2,200 dinar per month before deductions). But the elite is living in luxury... The danger of an uprising and a government overthrow is very high here, with all of the inevitable consequences.

There is also a high danger of epidemics, because people here are not in a hurry to take care of their health (the antibiotics are expensive). In addition, the sanitary conditions are revolting; in particular, the cities accumulate mountains of trash.

We live in a seismically active zone and have to take into consideration the likelihood of earthquakes. So...

These days we are consciously striving for independence, based on our life goals, plans, investments, and even the upbringing of our children. (I say "we" because I cannot talk about my life as separate from my husband's and my children's.)

Unfortunately, my more distant relatives are closed to such discussions, which they consider "extremist." And that's considering we are still quite far from being an ideal survivalist family! No matter what, we are talking about a purely personal approach, because, in spite of convincing arguments, people are often not ready to hear the truth. In spite of that, the evacuation of the French from Algiers was quite real!

When it comes to participating in making preparations, my participation is probably more pronounced than my husband's, because he works a lot and simply doesn't have the time to do everything at once. But he supports me in my decisions and is moving forward together with me, in the same direction. For example, right now we are building a more spacious garage, because we want to convert the former workshop into storage space, and construct a new workshop right in the garage. We are also taking steps toward buying four hectares of land not far from us, because our rural escape is a five hour drive from where we live and it is hard for us to go there regularly. We made a choice in favor of a plot of land in a rural setting, no more than an hour and a half away. Moreover, in two years (if catastrophe doesn't strike) we will pay off the mortgage on our house and will try to sell it, in order to buy a smaller house in town, and invest the remainder of the money in other plots of land. So, we have lots of projects! My husband is conservative when it comes to weapons. (He is a surgeon! Could this be professional distaste?) But I've been working on him for a year now. I think that he will apply for a gun permit soon. The proof of this is in the fact that I have in my possession documents that define the rules for gun ownership in Morocco.

Our expenditures are defined by our plans. I economize a lot by cooking at home, avoiding trips to restaurants, mending children's clothing, reusing many things many times, and buying the vitally important things before the simply necessary ones. But most importantly, I don't buy anything excessive (I am not a fashion victim!). When it comes to my children, here there is just one principle: gifts on Christmas and on birthdays, but that's it! When I buy things, I buy just one, but of high quality, instead of three that are all "Made in China." for example, my elder son's clothes were worn by his younger brothers, and the same thing can be said of toys, books...

As far as expenditures, we pay attention to how much water we consume. We bought a Class A washing machine that takes 8 kg loads (for a family of five this is not a luxury). We consider how much electricity we use (we have a solar water heater). I also pay attention to gasoline consumption and avoid unnecessary trips.

If I want to treat myself, I buy myself a small piece of gold jewelry. After all, this is also an investment!

When it comes to free time—and I haven't worked since June of 2012—I use it to go through our stockpiles and put them in order at least twice a week. On weekends we often take the children and drive out to nature, go on long walks. We teach them the basics of bushcraft (lighting fires, finding shelter, food, orienteering). For them this is a game. But they already have basic medical knowledge, which they received from me and my husband.

At the moment we can survive autonomously for three months. I am waiting until we have some more space in order to lay in some additional stores of food and various first-order necessities.

While the children are in school, I read a lot, in order to master the main techniques and the theory of autonomy, in order to live in accordance with the principles of autarky.

In everyday life I try to make practical use of all of my knowledge.

This takes a lot of energy, but it's also like a hobby. And this means that, in the final analysis, I am doing it for pleasure, and I am making use of my time in beneficial ways, while the children are in school! The only time there is stress is where you cannot cope with a crisis situation. But if you are prepared for, and especially if you are aware of what has to happen, you can control the situation. That's what I think.

Here are my priorities:

1. Stockpiling sufficient amount of food and first-order necessities; it is essential to supply yourself autonomously for at least a year.

2. Buying a house that is autonomous in terms of energy and water.

3. Buying a plot of land; otherwise it is impossible to eat autonomously!

4. Mastering various trades (baker, butcher, herbalist, gardner, veterinarian, cobbler, metalworker, etc.) depending one your abilities. For example, I don't see myself as a stonemason, but to work with wood, as a finishing carpenter... why not? And I love to make things!

5. Self-defense (we already have a crossbow and a dog!).

6. Read, read, and read some more.

7. To do things with your own hands, to put theory into practice, and to experiment. My husband loves to do this. He

already built solar water heaters, both in town and in "the wilderness." He is also refitting a yacht, which he bought cheaply from the customs office, fixing a car, doing a bit of gardening... Of course, only when he has time. Right now he is constructing a Stirling engine[116] together with the eldest son!

8. To convey our knowledge to our children.

Most important are the skills in producing and preserving food. When it comes to us personally, it is quite possible that at some point our profession will depend on our ability to treat ourselves without medications, only with medicinal plants.

In all: my husband is working like a slave, earning money, so that in the future we could invest it in something concrete (a plot of land, a house, etc.) and to survive without debt, and also to have more supplies. I do two-thirds of preparation work by myself. I resemble an orchestra conductor! Because I have more time! Again, I have no idea how it is possible to live for survivalists who have children and who both work.

When it comes to stockpiles, this is simple. I always put products with longer shelf life further away, and use the ones that are closer. Before buying something, I read the labels. If the products have a short shelf life, we try to use them up faster. Whenever we open a large container, I mark the date when it was opened on the lid.

When I see a good, high-quality product at a large (say, 50 percent) discount, I buy it without hesitation!

---

116 The Stirling engine, invented in 1916, runs on hot gas. It is a four-cycle engine: constant-volume heating, isothermic (constant-temperature) expansion, constant-volume cooling and isothermic compression. It was at first called a "warm-air engine" but was subsequently renamed because there is another type of engine that works on warm air.

When it comes to money, I sort it out in envelopes. One envelope for future expenditures, another—for large purchases (for example, a roof rack for the car).

Our children are still too small to participate fully in preparations, but the eldest son already knows how to behave, that we need to maintain a stockpile, how to defend ourselves in case of a fire or an earthquake. He knows what he should eat in order to always remain in good physical shape, knows about hygiene (washing his hands, blowing his nose). I have to say, I have been very lucky with my children. They are very highly developed and are doing well in school (and they do not have constant access to television!). My eldest son is already better than me in ornithology and astronomy. I think that he is going to be a good hunter. He has a crossbow (a toy, but quite effec-tive) and he makes his own arrows. They are not that good yet. But you have to start somewhere. We told him about a future without oil, and he is literally obsessed with defending the en-vironment. And he invents so many things! He wants to invent an engine that runs on air... He has mathematical abilities. Re-cently I talked to him about the possibility that we may have to leave the house quickly. And he packed a backpack just in case! The younger ones followed his example, thinking that this is a game. This allowed me to understand what they con-sider most valuable for themselves. I am teaching them to work in the garden and in the kitchen. This may turn out to be useful. This is how I convey my knowledge to them. This is very important, so that in the future our children will be able to find a way out of any situation.

Our way of life changed gradually. We were compelled to do this, because we didn't want to depend on the system! Of course, we didn't do this all at once, as an entire family, be-cause each of us had to adapt to the extent of their abilities... But since I am in charge, I set the overall tone. We care about our things, because we want them to serve us for a long time. I am investing in the future.

The most difficult thing for us was to change our free time, our vacations... But now we no longer have a choice. In any case, to breathe fresh air—that's good already...

I don't discuss this subject freely with those around me. I try to touch on various questions without entering into polemics, but often people don't have the information, and the conversation turns out to be useless... I have a woman-friend whom I am trying to acquaint with this subject matter in un-obtrusive ways... In any case, she has already been through a lot, that is prompting her to move in this direction. I sincerely think that one has to gather a certain amount of life experi-ence in order to understand these strivings, or to pick them up on one's youth together with someone else who is moving in the same direction. It is easier for me to talk to men, who are always aware of events, politics, economics...

What do we do in case of serious troubles? This problem worries me a lot! It's been a few months since I started con-vincing my husband to buy a rifle. We have put together an evacuation plan, having consulted a map. We intend to reach our shelter over a minor road. Since it is far from us, we are planning to buy a plot of land nearby... However, our "wilder-ness" has certain advantages: my husband is a member of a large group of friends that are very helpful to each other. And since he is a surgeon, he commands a great deal of respect and everybody is willing to help him. I think that we will be safe (up in the mountains everybody is armed!).

Besides that, our house is located in a modest neighborhood (in times of troubles, there will be frequent burglaries). It is located far from the exit from the city. All of our neighbors are hunters, and all of them have relatives who live along the way to our "wilderness." Even though we have a guard dog, there are grilles on all the windows. The entrance door is steel-plated. This is better than nothing!

I am trying to teach our eldest son to defend himself. As far as the younger children, I understand perfectly well that without us their chances of survival are nil.

I believe that our "striving for independence" is equally characteristic of women as of men. Especially if they are responsible for the children. I'll say more: in a crisis situation a woman becomes the first victim. Don't we see that in countries where there is war or chaos women are in an unenviable position? Rapes, illegal imprisonment, brothels for the soldiers, torture, blackmail with threats against husbands and relatives, sexual slavery... In our days we are confronted with numerous examples of all of this: Syria (psychological warfare conducted by both sides), Sudan, Darfour, Afghanistan, Colombia, Mexico, India, Iran... Even Morocco and France... Women and children become the first victims of conflicts and crisis situations. But when you know about your vulnerability, you must do everything you can to compensate for it. This is what needed to be proven!

To a woman who is just starting out, I would recommend that she first do some reading and collect information, and only then embark on preparations. I think that all survivalists have passed through period when they doubted everything, because of their reading and their conversations among themselves. But you can't form your own opinions without becoming acquainted with various well-argued theses and anti-theses... Then, if she becomes convinced, I would advise her to put together an EDC kit. This is very easy for a woman, who always has her purse with her!

You also have to organize and equip your dwelling, and make it safe not just from fire, but from burglars, etc.

Then I would acquaint her with my priorities (which I enumerated above). We would discuss priorities, which she will select for herself, in accordance with her personal economic situation. I will share my knowledge with her, and will always be ready to come to her aid...

I think that many men have a distorted view of women. But this is an endless topic of discussion... But seriously, women obviously have lower muscle mass (except for sportswomen and fitness fanatics). But we are often more perceptive and more inventive then men. If, when my eldest son was born, I depended solely on my husband, we would have had just a set of pajamas and a bottle! With cow's milk! Of course, he has taken care of hundreds of children, but "the details are a woman's domain." So says my dear, caring husband... Luckily for myself and my son, for whom today he sets an example, he has a very smart wife (he says so himself!) who enlightened him before the birth of our child. This is a banal but convincing example.

I think that men should see a woman not as an inconvenient hindrance but as an additional resource, the main one in a crisis situation... Acting alone, a man would not be able to cope with everything, especially if he has children.

A severe crisis situation can go on for a long time, but then what? Men have to prepare for a future together with us. Otherwise there won't be any life, just surviving!

We cannot be compared. So what if we have two eyes, mouth, brain, just like men, but we use them differently. And this is a trump card, and not any sort of shortcoming! We must respect ourselves and listen to ourselves.

We, women, can display amazing psychic and physical power, which can sometimes surpass that of men. There are convincing examples of this. When they observe a birth, many fathers faint. And they are supposed to defend us? And is it really just men who fight during wars and revolutions? Is it really just men who act bravely? Do women not work in "difficult" professions?

Yes, many women will panic, because they are unprepared. But the same thing can be said of their unprepared brothers.

In conclusion, I would like to say this: never underestimate an enraged woman who is defending her "nest"!

The process of translating the theory of survival into practice is moving forward full steam ahead... Our workshop is almost finished, our supplies increase every week, soon we will buy a plot of land nearby. We have converted the few savings we had into gold bars. Our children ate all the strawberries we raised in our garden. Now every day they will be harvesting radishes, and my husband is reading your Mean Streets. Yesterday he bought two large bags of fine sand (for water filtration)... Our yacht is in the water and has passed a sea trial. Now we just have to varnish it and set up the cabin. Our neighbor is teaching us to shoot, because there is no shooting club nearby. We are shooting old-style: at tin cans!

In short... It takes time to create a new way of life. We hope that we have enough of it, so that nothing catches us un-awares!

Anne

"In our quiet village corner we listen to silence."

My name is Anne, I am married, and I have two sons, aged 27 and 23. Right now I am working as a household aid for a sick elderly lady.

A few years ago my husband and I decided to find a place to live in a village, to get some rest and, most importantly, to prepare for a way of life based on the principles of autarky, because we are becoming more and more convinced that in the nearest future the situation in the world will get worse, and that we will encounter numerous serous problems: financial, political, climate, anger and violence, wars... All of this has forced us to start thinking. And so for four years already we have been making various efforts. We are practicing Christians, we read the Bible and we are particularly interested in the prophesies of Daniel and the Book of Revelation. In talking with our friends, who are also Christian, we have come to the conclusion that our world is on the threshold of serious upheavals and that, in the end, Jesus the Son of God will come to us, to finish off all the evil that has reigned for so long on the earth.

We are convinced that financial collapse will come sooner or later. And what will city-dwellers do then, who depend on the system—that is, on drinking water, salaries, bank accounts, food in the supermarkets, medical help, consequences of environmental pollution, danger of pandemics that require immediate vaccination, on declarations of a state of emergency that is quite likely in case of a popular revolt, and so on?

But we are not panicking, and every day we are moving forward. A year ago my husband lost his job. He received severance pay, and now he is collecting unemployment benefits. We are compelled to move forward by our faith. We trust in God and we have no fear. We sold our house, which was conveniently located on the outskirts of Geneva. Everything happened quickly. Our house, which is 24 years old, sold very quickly. And without any regrets we invested the money in a house in a village, which stands apart from the rest, in order to shelter there when everything starts falling apart.

Right now our priority is tilling the earth. We are preparing it, in order to be able to grow our own vegetables this coming spring. We are testing how well our source of water is working, and making a stockpile of foodstuffs with long shelf life. We are planning to bake our own bread (we want to build an oven for baking cakes and pizzas), to make jams and preserves, to can vegetables. My husband is very well-organized. He spends every day on preparing and organizing. He does everything with a good attitude and a prayer. Any time I have the opportunity I join him, because our homestead is a seven-hour drive from the house where we are currently living (I work in Geneva). We have made a big stockpile of firewood for heating and installed a wood-burning stove with an oven for cooking. It also warms the house! We are happy.

Right now our food stockpile is stored in a small shed. But we want to transfer it to a cellar with an earthen floor which is located below the freeze zone.

Our relatives and friends are full of admiration for us and understand our motivations perfectly. When the time comes, they will also be involved in the process of preparing... We have many friends who know about our hopes and plans. All of them are fully engaged in thinking about the necessity of preparing and want to follow our example.

Living in this cruel world, we understand well that we can become victims of looters, extortionists and thieves. But in spite of all this we preserve our tranquility, because our guardian angels are looking out for us. We place all of our trust and our faith in the Lord God, our Creator.

We do not have weapons with which to defend ourselves. Our territory is surrounded by a simple mesh fence. We have done everything humanly possible to isolate ourselves, and have installed a large gate. And in everything else we rely on God's mercy.

As a woman, a wife and a mother I support my husband 100 percent. I do the gardening, and I urge other women to start doing the same as son as possible. In our little rural corner we listen to silence, to birds singing early in the morning, we breathe clean air. There are no nuclear power plants or factories nearby. We are surrounded by five hectares [12 acres] of forest and meadow. Our life has taken on a new meaning. Gradually, unhurriedly, we are reconstructing true human values. All the money we earn we immediately invest in essential supplies. We no longer keep money in a bank account, because money will soon lose its value. We have thought it all through.

I call upon women to seriously think about the possibility of leaving the city and settling down in a village. Women should try to influence their life's partners, so that they start to see things differently, because we are facing hard times.

I also advise you to join efforts with kindred spirits, with resourceful people and, if possible, to pool money, knowledge, good will and, most importantly, trust, belonging and faith. Children who grow up in a village are defended from violence and bad influences.

As far as the men who are reading this book, I call on them to get their families out of the cities as soon as possible, and to alter their life's direction, because nothing can compare with freedom, tranquility and, most importantly, independence!

If you don't have enough money to buy a house, you can rent it for a ten-year period or find a position as a caretaker on a farm.

Caroline

"We are not the lowest race!"

I am 29 years old, I am French, and I am in a long-term relationship with a woman. I live in a village, in a small commune
that has 2,000 members. I have no children. I raise aquacul-
ture. I love handcrafts, nature, fishing. For three years now
I've been doing karate and marksmanship. I work as a volunteer in one of the civil defense organizations.

In 2010, while I was searching the internet for information
about marksmanship and rifles, I accidentally came across Vol
West's web site. At first, after I scanned the articles, I said to
myself: "Here is another person who glorifies weapons while
waiting for the world to end." Then I read one of the articles
that caught my eye more carefully. I liked it. I decided to look
at some other articles. And I realized that I had been entirely
wrong about this author. He wrote very accessibly on subject
that seemed obvious to me. In reality, I was unconsciously a
survivalist my whole life, in my own way, and this blog opened
my eyes. It is the fault of the mass media, and our own ignorance, that we have a distorted view of what it means to be a
survivalist. In our imagination it's someone who is armed to
the teeth, locked up in his bunker, absolutely asocial. I had also
been in the grip of this cliché, even though I was open to
learning new things. Luckily, the theory and practice of survivalism have nothing to do with such whimsy.

The situation in the world is growing progressively worse:
crises, layoffs, shortages of food, more and more serious natural disasters and so on. I would like to say that Vol West's blog

has served as a starting point for me and, possibly, has prompted me to become a property owner and to start thinking about my future.

For me the greatest risk in the future will of course be loss of employment; that is, being fired for economic reasons. The enterprise where I work breeds oysters and sells oyster larvae. Since we are working with living beings, we have to confront a high level of mortality because of many factors that don't depend on us and which we cannot control. Once we lost half of our production, which was all ready to ship. And so, it is impossible for us to foresee the future. That's exactly why, in case of difficult and testing times, I maintain a supply of food.

I have to say, I was always drawn to the idea of independence and autonomy. I gained a great deal of knowledge thanks to the internet and to books. Books help me preserve in my memory facts that I have learned and to return to them if I have doubts or if I forget something. I often tell myself: "Look, this might come in handy!" or "How can I use this thing again?"

In a certain sense this is positive stress. I know that there are things which I cannot buy or make because of my financial situation and other limitations. But this causes me to look for alternative solutions that lead to autonomy.

A part of my free time is spent preparing, while trying not to sacrifice my relationship or cut into my free time. But sometimes I don't have enough courage and energy to prepare. Also, it's important that preparing doesn't turn into an obsession. As far as the budget, things are not so simple. We work on two salaries that are only slightly higher than the legal minimum that is set in France. We have recently built a house in which we have been living for a year and a half now. Unfortunately, we were forced to take out a 25-year mortgage. We had no opportunity to become property owners without going into debt. We try to economize for the sake of our house. After construction is complete there are always many things left over (the yard, the kitchen garden, small chores). We also prepare, but this is not easy. In the summer I have additional work, and so I can set some money aside for a rainy day.

It is very important for me to perfect my skills in the so-called manual disciplines. I feel a vital need to do everything on my own, to not have to summon specialists to deal with trivial problems. To fix a headlight or a car tire, to clean out a gutter, to repair furniture, to make something for the household... These are all trivial things for me. But many women (and even some men) are incapable of doing such things with their own hands. Of course, there are also things of which we are incapable. For example, for me this is electricity, which, I have to admit, strikes fear into my heart. Nevertheless, I will try to learn at least the basics. I am lucky that I love to make things. My father taught me many things when I was still a child. It is very important to know your way around nature: to know the types of trees, plants, to learn to fish, hunt and so on. It is also essential to be less dependent on sources of energy and food. We bought a wood-burning stove, and this allowed us to heat the house. We are planning a kitchen-garden, and then we will learn to do canning.

Each month we set money aside for buying food for storage, gasoline and a few silver bars. This is not a precisely defined budget; it is set approximately. As far as everything else, we first buy what we need to assure our independence, whenever we can.

When it comes to distributing tasks between us, most of the time this turns out to be 50-50. When it comes to making things, here I have greater aptitude than my partner.

I place a lot of emphasis on questions of economy and re-use. For example, it is important not too spend too long in the shower, to drive less aggressively, never to throw away food scraps (save them until next time, or put them in the compost) ... I can say that all of this has made me more mature, forced me to recognize life's hardships. I also understood how little it takes for life to fall apart, that life is not some long, calm river, and that it is impossible to live immersed in utopia. I am not a pessimist; I am a realist.

The most difficult thing for me was not to get organized but to realize that I lack the financial resources to do everything to achieve total independence.

Nobody knows that I am a survivalist, with the exception of my partner, of course, who walks alongside me on this path. I don't dare speak of this with strangers, because I know (or think that I know) how people will relate to it. They don't have the openness of mind to understand us. Of course, a few people know that I do composting on my own, but that's about it. As far as they are concerned, I am something like an ecologist. This suits me just fine. If I see that people are trying to under-stand me, I talk to them about various subjects. But if I see that they don't approve of me, I don't insist on my point of view.

But if you listen to their conversations, you find out that they are also a little bit like survivalists. They just don't know that they are! I remember how one time at work we were talk-ing about the end of the world that was supposed to happen on

December 21, 2012. My colleagues mentioned some survivalists that they saw on television. For them these survivalists were maniacs, deprived of social connections and fixated on their isolation. It is very difficult to explain to people that mass media do not always reflect the truth. But people are much more tolerant of the word "independence," even though independence and survivalism are closely connected. Possibly, they regard the word "survivalism" as pejorative? When you are living in a comfortable setting, when you don't know what war is, which my grandfathers and grandmothers experienced, and who were in essence survivalists, then you don't think about any of that, and feel safe.

Preparation is very important for a woman. The situation in the world is getting worse, and we can see that. So we can't be simple-minded. There are numerous examples that show us that the system is working badly, that it is not always able to help us (hurricane Katrina, Fukushima, the crisis in Greece, the unreliability of the banks and so on). Unfortunately, the population is always forced to make sacrifices in order to try to save this unstable system, which is profitable for the powerful of this world (banks, governments, multinational corporations...). The less we depend on them, the less vulnerable we are going to be.

I think that women should also want to be more independent of men, not to lean on their shoulders. We are able to do the same things that they are. I don't want to sound like a feminist, but I consider it important to show that we are not some lower race, that women can be independent.

If I get the opportunity to give advice to a woman, this advice will be based on my personal experience. Then I will recommend to her to gather all the information she can on the internet or to get it out of books. You have to start with things that suit you the best, and which bring pleasure. And don't get fixated on any one thing. You have to try to find out what suits you specifically.

As far as men, let them be tolerant and open, and let them agree that we have the same abilities. Everyone has their own experience, and we all possess knowledge. We can share it and complete each other. As they say, unity creates power. In the process of preparing, we occupy the same proper place as they do.

Fanny

"This difficult life has made me strong."

In answering your questions, I want to say that I really think that women, especially those with families, should have a more developed survivalist instinct than men, first because we are physically weaker, and this is a fact, and second because we are internally connected to our children. But I sincerely think that parents are making a mistake: now, if a woman has children, she no longer teaches them to do anything with their own hands! I grew up in a special family and for me survivalism is in my blood.

My Name is Fanny, I am 27 years old, a practicing Catholic, married and a mother. Right now I am on maternity leave and spend all my time caring for my infant. As far as my life's path, I am a woman who grew up in a difficult environment. This allowed me to understand very early on that there are evil people and that you must try not to become their victim.

This also connected me with such incredible women as prostitutes. They certainly know life! And they maintain a good grip on men's balls. They were the only ones who agreed to hide me and my mother when we ran away from our home, which had become dangerous for us. Annie, the woman who saved us, gave us a gold coin as a parting present, so that we would have a way to counter any difficulty. At the time gold had real value... I was brought up based on a simple principle: "Help yourself, and the heavens will help you." My father had an eloquent tattoo on his leg: "Walk or die." My father wanted a son, but life turned out otherwise. When I was six I already

190

knew how to use his metal lathe, hammer together little boats out of wooden splints, and I had no problems when he asked me to hand him the 5mm wrench.

At the same time I resembled other girls who were dreaming of Barbie dolls. But this difficult life made me strong. I gradually turned into the sort of woman I am today: competent, feminine, vigilant, but getting pleasure out of life at every moment.

You will laugh, but the idea of becoming a survivalist came to me in the bathroom. It was my mother's bathroom. She had an old copy of the comic book *The Junior Woodchucks* lying around there. I decided that this is a very useful comic book, and started to look for similar works written for adults. This is how I came across a survivalist manual. After reading it, I bought our first EDC kit, not knowing yet where this will lead me. Then I started doing searches for "survivalism" on Google and came across Vol West's blog. I was stunned! That was the beginning of everything. Since then I read a lot. I understood that I must prepare, and quickly!

To tell you the truth, I believe that our society, in its current state (economic, political) is at risk of collapse, and that this will lead to numerous tragedies. And the process is continuously accelerating!

My priority is to have a roof over my head that's free and clear![117] You know what they say: "Let it be small, but your own than big and somebody else's." It is important to have skills and know-how. I value well-rounded people, McGuyvers, and I hope to become one myself. In any case, that's what I am aiming for. It is enough to place a goal before yourself and to

117 That is, unencumbered by any debts.

have a minimum of abilities... I want to underscore the ability to do things—this is good, but knowing how to live is the most important. Try to remain on the right side of the barrier, no matter what happens. Don't let your heart grow hard, that's the most important thing!

I prepare each and every moment. This is my way of life and my way of thinking. I don't feel stress, because we acquired our own SAB quite quickly, which was vitally important for us. I work on preparing when my baby is asleep. As far as the budget, we calculate it every month. Sometimes we allow ourselves to relax!

It is very important to invest in preparing every day. Let somebody think that this is stupid, but I feel my responsibility as the mother of the family, and in the evenings I check the contents of the backpacks with things and food for the baby and always leave clothing in the hallway close to the door. Bags packed in case of evacuation are located close to our beds. And so, everything is ready if we have to leave suddenly in the middle of the night. Think about the miserable people who were caught unprepared when the rivers overflowed their banks![118] They were left with absolutely nothing!

As far as food stockpiles, we store a stockpile of water and food in the apartment to last us a week, and in case of evacuation we have supplies for two more weeks. In our SAB we will be able to live autonomously for two months. But our weakest link is the water. We need a lot of water, and it is heavy. I renew our supply regularly. Yes, a lot of it is needed every day. It is much more difficult to rotate the stock of medicines. When

---

118 She is talking about the floods that struck the southwest of France in 2013.

they expire we have to throw them out. As far as cash, I won't talk about it. Our tasks are distributed as follows: I scan the blogs and various articles on the internet, in order to find out how to prepare better, watch the financial and political news and compile lists of what remains to be done. My husband does the heavy work that requires physical strength. But most importantly he stays fit, to be able to defend us in case of catastrophe.

This way of life forces us to always be two steps ahead, to remain informed about current events in the world, to listen carefully to them. In the beginning the most difficult thing was for us to "swallow the red pill," as in the move *The Matrix*; then we encountered a shortage of financial resources. We never have the money to do everything all at once. That's why we have to do everything gradually.

I value the opinion of my family and friends. We want to pass on the message, to urge people to collect information for themselves, to have their own opinion. But except for two people, nobody wants to "swallow the red pill"... so far. One of the people who are close to me even let me know that he thinks that I joined a sect! I felt insulted. Honestly, this shows how little he knows me, and how little he values my intelligence!

If normal life collapses, I hope that we will be sufficiently prepared to provide for the safety of our family. I am Catholic, but I want to be clear: I don't recommend anyone who tries to attack us to go anywhere near me, because I will give him the works!

About our child, here everything is clear. The child must remain in a child's world. Of course, we will bring him up with the logic of autonomy and respect for those who are close. I don't walk around in a gas mask with a baseball bat, I am a perfectly normal mother. But in my purse I have a flashlight Fenix® E05, a Leatherman® multitool, and pepper spray... all of that, in a pink satin bag. A woman's EDC kit; so what?

I am not a feminist, not at all, but it is important to be as independent as possible. That's not my case at all, but every day I am becoming more and more independent.

To my female friends I will say this: "Collect information, prepare and, most importantly, remain feminine, because your husband will support you, and nothing is keeping you from being elegant and, at the same time, a survivalist."

Men, remember that behind every great man stands a woman.

Isabelle

"They want to live in a world thought
up by Disney!"

I want to warn you right away: I am not speaking on behalf
of women, just on behalf of myself. In all, I find that the words
of people who have claimed for themselves the right to speak
on someone else's behalf are completely useless and inevitably
turn into a caricature: male chauvinism, violence and lack of
courtesy for some; the image of the victim, inescapable
"women's intuition" and revanchist anger on the other.

I always try to avoid such clichés, because men and women
are condemned to cooperate and agree with each other (and,
in addition, to love...) even if they don't always understand
each other! However, there exist certain obvious differences:
men have greater physical strength, which is very significant
for survival; they have a thirst for adventure and, consequently, a more inquisitive mind. I don't think that there are
differences on the intellectual level. Women are just as intelligent as men... and women are just as stupid as men.

I was born in 1960, in a middle-class family. My father was
the director of a factory. In the end of 1960 he opened an ad-
vertising agency. Business was going well. I had a carefree
childhood and an exciting youth in the 1980s, when I attended
acting classes in Paris. This was a period of great freedom,
when it was easy to remake the world having read some book.
I am a graphic artist and decorator (frescoes, trompe l'oeil,
etc.) but I have so little work that it's scaring me. I read a lot,
and I sometimes write (humorous sketches). I am bringing up

my son alone. He is currently 17.

I had not just one but several motivations, in series, which prompted me to move forward:

I was in mourning for someone dear to me. That was the first stage, when I felt for the first time that I was "surviving."

The birth of my son (a huge feeling of responsibility, stronger because I was bringing him up alone, while my financial condition began to worsen).

A break with my family, because of which I was forced to seek a way out of my situation on my own.

And... the influence of mass media, which every day seemed to lie more and more, idle wanderings, reading, lectures, internet searches, Piero's books and Vol West's blog to sum it all up (yes, indeed!).

I consider an economic collapse to be most probable, connected with the depletion of energy resources, overpopulation and the incompetence of our elite (among other things). I am already beginning to feel the effect of all of these negative aspects on myself. But, of course, all the worst is still to come. I follow the news in various ways: mainstream media, which explains to me what is being said and what I ought to think about (otherwise I wonder why I would ever turn on the television), as well as other sources. I don't fence myself off against anything, I listen to everything, then sift through it. I think that the crisis will give rise to violence. If the people who are living under anesthesia (movies, government aid and so on) wake up with a sharp pain, then they, unable to see any sort of future, are at great risk of becoming very angry.

Here is a ranking of my fears:

No. 1: The lack of a wall = helplessness in the face of violence = my main worry: defense. I have started to learn how to shoot and I plan to buy one or two types of firearms. At the present moment I am not able to create an SAB (I had a house but I lost it two years ago in divorce). But this is very important. This causes great worry for me (thinking about my son) along with my isolation.

Other risks associated with the crisis: a totalitarian and corrupt government. I will escape from here to the "free zone," as in 1940. Another scenario: escape to Québec, where I have friends. I just have to buy tickets on time! Or... there is no other solution, except to force everyone to forget about me and try to preserve a certain amount of freedom...

No. 2: Climatic cataclysms: you have to listen to Jean-Marc Jancovici,[119] who is an expert on climatology and energy. This is more than probable, but with unpredictable consequences... In such a scenario I have no Plan B.

No. 3: Bacteriological, chemical or other type of war. No plan. I just have to keep as far away from the cities as possible.

No. 4: Catastrophe, nuclear war: wait it out, shut in a bunker, in constant fear, loneliness or crowded conditions—that's not for me. Even if I have such a possibility, in order to maintain my will to live I need beauty, kindness and hope. Otherwise—forget it! I have to face death with as much dignity as possible.

Now I am convinced that preparing should be my main concern. This is at the same time a consolation (because I am not the only one who thinks so; many people believe in the possibility of chaos), and also a source of stress, because I realize

119 See www.manicore.com.

how financially helpless I am in terms of preparation, and also incapable of convincing my old friends and my family. And so, I am forced to put together an emergency kit for my son while only hinting at what I am doing. Many people associate such actions with paranoia, and then take us to be cult members, pessimists who live in expectation of catastrophe, or even fascists! In my free time I study. If I find out about alternative sources of energy, then blackouts won't be a problem for me. Budget? Yes, budget... This was never my strong suit. Running the household... I do everything in a burst of enthusiasm, giving priority to this or that direction!

In a word, I have an EDC kit, two emergency kits, knowledge that I gained by attending lectures, one or two firearms that I plan to acquire, a month's worth of food (provided my son doesn't eat too much), a first aid kit... At the moment that's all there is. As far as social connections, I am trying to develop acquaintances. This is happening gradually, and rather slowly, because that's how it works here. But considering what is bound to happen (economic crisis) I give priority to the SAB, trying to convert my dwelling into it. I would like to keep animals (chickens), to grow vegetables, to find a solution for generating electricity, to be minimally autonomous in terms of electricity, to be closer to a source of water. But at the moment I still can't do that, because I live in an apartment in Paris. However, I already started to grow vegetables on my balcony!

What kinds of knowledge do I consider important? First: grow food, hunt, take care of my health, learn to defend myself and make various things. What I know: how to grow certain plants, how to care for horses and ride them, ride a motorcycle, sail (a little), I am learning how to shoot, I can give injections and administer first aid, I like to tell children about the ancient monuments of our culture, I cook, I draw, I can sew a little... As far as everything else, I follow the course of events and quickly learn everything. There is one thing that isn't knowledge or a skill, but I think that it's important: you have to adapt quickly. I deal with everything on my own, because I live alone with my son. As far as money, that's very simple: every month I walk on knife's edge!

In essence, my lifestyle hasn't changed in any fundamental way, unless you consider certain new types of activity. But my vision of the future has changed considerably. You can say that if I realized this before, I would have made a different choice, specifically as far as my son's upbringing and education. My main difficulties are connected with the lack of money and the lack of understanding from those close to me, which sometimes condemn me to solitude and give rise to a feeling of helplessness. In spite of the crisis, which is obvious, those close to me consider me a pessimist, panicky and crazed. They have started to visit me more rarely. I like my friends very much, but they can't be bothered to start doing research, to gather information, to think, to understand. They are very sweet, but they are incorrigible Parisians, socially secure, artists, leftists, humanists... We walk different paths. I feel that they want to live in a world invented by Walt Disney, where everyone is so kind. I am not angry at them, because previously I used to think (only sometimes!) just like them. It makes me sad to realize that an abyss is gradually opening up between us.

Each person must try to achieve, to the greatest extent possible, independence from the system and from others. By her nature, a woman is more vulnerable and less independent, if she has children. Children are a woman's Achilles' heel, because she tries to avoid risk for their sake, worrying about their well-being. In my opinion, a childless woman is just as free as a man. If she becomes dependent, that's because she wants to.

As far as weapons, here I am speaking as a "typical woman": it is very difficult for me to imagine that I will wield a blade. As far as hand-to-hand combat... hmm... Yes, of course, you never know ahead of time, but I don't feel that I am capable of tackling an enraged maniac, face to face. As far as passive defenses —barbed wife, alarm and so on—I have all of that. I calm myself thinking that we have a strong door!

To the men who are reading this I would like to say the following: don't underestimate the bravery of women during a crisis, rely on them as on genuine partners if you consider them as such. But do not overestimate them. They are not at all like Rambo. Take care of your children, nurture them. This will reassure them. That's exactly what it means to be a man: to defend your wife and children. And continue to treat us as women, with respect and tenderness.

Katya

"In the word 'survival' I hear the word 'life.'"

What about me? I am married, a computer repair technician and I help with the household. I don't have any children yet, but I have two dogs, two cats, two chickens and we are planning to get a goat! Our point of departure? Once a friend came to me and gave me a book: *How to Survive Economic Collapse.* I read it in a single night, and it overwhelmed me. Since then my husband has started noticing that I am changing. He also gained the same understanding and has started to prepare, gradually, in his own rhythm. Even before I bought a lot of books with practical advice in them, but now I buy even more of them. I have a certain understanding of economics, and so this book allowed me to glimpse new horizons. Before I allowed myself to relax. Now, though this may seem strange, I have faith in the future, because I have faith in myself. I know that life's difficulties are real and can happen in any area. It is better to come to terms with this idea. I always wanted to be independent from the system. I live in a village, although I work in a big city. I like to till the earth and to take care of animals. We have to pay a lot of money to the workers we hire, and so I found a second job.

Since we work a lot we don't have much free time. I prepare more than my husband. I ask him to look over our supplies and to read some practical guides... I am teaching him to cook, to garden, to sew. He appreciates all of this. He is worried about his country and about his job. But I worry more about our relatives. I show things to them and sometimes present them with survivalist "fetishes" such as water filters, first aid kits and so on. They are delighted! I am very interested in old-fashioned skills and know-how. I love handcrafts (crochet, sewing, knitting), and I have mastered the basics of carpentry, furniture restoration, because I have relatives who work in these fields. For two years I traded in used things. My parents are very skilled. I often see how they make something. And I, as a rule, do all the work around the home.

Previously I thought that I should live as other women: watch television, go out, follow fashion... Now I have decided to first of all concern myself with myself and with those close to me. Everything else is useless and annoys me. I don't like to go to the city too often. Of course, I am happy to meet people, but I foresee and already feel increasing social pressure on myself.

It is very important for me to know the opinions of others, especially those of people who are close to me. We need them. They are a reflection of our selves, but we must not forget what we hold in the depths of our own souls. On my way toward independence I stockpile water, fuel, cans of food. This brings me relief. On the other hand, the lack of food in the house causes me stress. I prefer to sleep less and not to watch television, but to regularly inventory our supplies. I gave away our electric sewing machine and bought another one at a liquidation, an old one, with a foot pedal. For ten years now I have been buying clothing at liquidation sales organized by the Red Cross. You can find high-quality things there! This has allowed me to save up a large sum of money. I reuse things, find them at liquidation sales, fix furniture and household objects. This allows me not just to save money but also to add to our budget. You have to live within your means. Then you have to develop that which can turn out to be useful. Put tools into your hands, and knowledge into your minds!

This striving for independence is really very important for me. In the word "survival" I hear the word "life." I often say to the people I love: "Take care of yourself." For me, that is everything! Being survivalists, we are practically defenseless. We have just our knowledge, supplies, tools and instruments, social connections. Preparing takes time. You have to keep it all in mind. Happy trails!

Melanie

"When you start talking about this, it gets easier."

To begin, let me briefly introduce myself. I live in Québec, I am over 30, married, mother of two adolescent girls, one small boy and one infant who will be born any moment now. We live in a remote spot, in a village surrounded by forest, in the very center of Gaspésie Provincial Park. Because we live so far from other population centers I teach my children at home, based on the school program. We discovered survivalist theory for ourselves approximately a year and a half ago thanks to the documentary film *Collapse*.[120] Then, in the following weeks, I read several books and watched several documentary films on this subject, to arrive at a fuller understanding. I didn't need a lot of time to get the idea. We don't have a large income, and we are moving forward in small steps. I think that we have secured our base, although there is a lot left for us to do. We dream of putting down deep roots (although we don't have any experience) but we have to work to do with what we have. This isn't so bad, because we live in a forest, close to sources of drinking water and far from large cities. We try to learn to cultivate crops, through trial and error, of course. But we must keep in mind that we are living in the mountains, in a very cold climate, so it's not so easy.

---

120 A documentary film featuring Michael Ruppert about the dangers of the crash of modern civilization due to natural resource depletion which was released in 2009.

I consider myself a "calm prepper." Of course, I only discuss this in my close circle, but I am not politicized and no more interested than the GI Joes I see in the other Québec residents (men, mostly). I believe in the importance of security, but I don't turn it into an obsession. I am more concerned about the well-being of my family, the people around me, my community. That's exactly the direction of my preparations: to supply those close to me with everything that's needed, and perhaps to alleviate people's suffering, when that becomes necessary.

My approach is strictly practical. For example, I am preparing a set of clothes for my children up to their adulthood. I use coupons for purchases in order to add to our food stockpile. I am putting together a library of useful books. We are trying to widen our practical knowledge. We encourage our children to do useful things in their spare time (knit, sew and so on). In a word, my concerns have an everyday, practical character.

In the beginning I didn't think that the economy could collapse. But, after reading many books and articles on this subject, I became convinced that this shockwave will reach even me. *Collapse*, the documentary film, shocked me so much that I couldn't sleep all night. I felt the need to find out more. Then I discovered The Crash Course by Chris Martenson[121] and bought and read the book *How to Survive the End of the World as We Know It* by James Rawles.[122] These works laid the foundation of my knowledge and convinced me of the importance of preparing. My entire universe shifted; after all, before I was traveling on a completely different path. My family even thought of returning to the city. But these works forced me to fundamentally re-

121 See www.peakprosperity.com.
122 See www.survivalblog.com.

examine my way of thinking. I have to admit, I was gripped by fear. But, being a practicing Christian, I quickly calmed down, as if the Holy Sprit brought me to my senses by telling me that everything will be all right. I think that this is exactly why I was able to see things rationally, and could forbid fear to control me.

Reading books and watching documentary films convinced me that our world is much more fragile than conventional wisdom tells us. I imagine that many things could happen, but in my opinion some are more probable than others. The most probable, it seems to me, are economic collapse (worldwide and national), shortage of natural resources (oil, minerals, etc.) on which our lifestyle is based. Then there is the possibility of epidemics (which were always cyclical throughout our history). Although the risk isn't great, I think that we may have to face another world war which can trigger a nuclear threat. On the local scale, we are not insured against natural cataclysms, which have become more frequent in recent years. In a word, I am mostly preparing for economic collapse of our system, with fundamental changes in our way of life. One way or another, any of these dangers can lead to the collapse of modern society.

During the first weeks of preparing I threw all of my energy into it, all of my time, all of my money. It's as if I fell into the opposite extreme. I didn't want to waste a single minute, a single dollar. I think that I was driven by fear, and also uncertainty, because I didn't know how much time was allotted to me. But since then I have regained my balance. However, I understand that I must constantly push myself, because it is easy to abstract yourself from the future and to return to the comfort of daily life. Now we devote a reasonable part of our time to preparing while continuing to lead normal lives. The same thing with money. Since I secured my SAB I feel more carefree. By this I mean to say that if tomorrow morning it all collapses, we will be able to survive, because we have a minimum of everything that's necessary (drinking water, warmth, food, security). Life will be difficult, but possible. And so, since the time when we secured our base, we have felt the need to bring our preparations and our current life into balance.

In order to find the money we need to prepare we try to live more humbly. For many years already I buy groceries using coupons, combining them with special sales. This allows me to buy more products and to create good stockpiles. We try to cook using fresh ingredients, we don't buy prepared food, and this allows us to save a lot of money. When fruits and vegetables are available at reasonable prices we buy them in bulk and can or dry them. This takes time, but it increases our supplies in an affordable fashion.

We prefer to buy used things, and fix and maintain the things we have whenever possible. For example, understanding that my three-year-old son will need clothes up to his adulthood, I visit clothing markets and thrift shops and buy at a discount clothing which he will wear in the future. As far as the time needed to do all this, there are problems. Of course, this demands absolute dedication from all of us. We have explained the current situation to our older daughters, and they understand why we are preparing. This helps us to involve them in the process of preparing. Everybody is supporting everybody else. This is the only way to make preparation possible. We shorten the time we allow for leisure, but we try not to eliminate it altogether. We try to direct our leisure toward practical pursuits, looking for activities that will later become beneficial. My daughters knit and sew. When walking in the forest we try to recognize what is around us and try to figure out what is edible and what isn't. This is very useful in the context of home-schooling. I would say that it is possible to find the time by changing our way of life, our activities and our leisure.

Our goal is complete autonomy. We don't know whether we will ever be able to achieve it, but we are headed in that direction. Our main priority is food. We have a good stockpile, and we are constantly adding to it. Our goal is to supply our family's needs for at least a year, which is long enough to survive until the next harvest and, if possible, enough to share with other families. In pursuing autonomy in food we are simultaneously learning other things, such as canning, drying, smoking, etc. We want to learn to produce things on our own, by gardening and, in the future, by keeping animals. We also want to learn to gather what nature offers. We live surrounded by forests, and the flora here is rich in most unexpected wild foods. We are interested in mycology and trying to learn how to fish, hunt and set traps.

After that come other priorities: to make it easier to get drinking water, to increase the stockpile of firewood, to develop a system of renewable energy, to accumulate things we might need in the future and which, quite possibly, it will become impossible to buy; to take the minimal precautions to avoid getting robbed.

We also feel that it is very important to establish contacts within our community and to enlighten our neighbors, to help them become independent.

Each of us has a list of tasks which we have to carry out every day in order for our household to function well. This order allows us to free up time to devote to unforeseen problems. Preparing is not necessarily a part of our everyday schedule; we do it cyclically—for example, when there is a bounty of cheap vegetables. I could say that we widen our schedule, but do so spontaneously. For example, one weekend may be devoted to canning, while others afford us more free time. When it comes to rotating stocks, the most important thing is organization and labeling. Otherwise chaos is quick to arrive, and can overwhelm us and make us lose hope.

We set the family budget together. We try to carve out the resources necessary for preparation. But most importantly, first and foremost, we try to get rid of debts.

We feel that we are living well, because together and in harmony we are moving toward a common goal.

The most important thing is that our way of thinking has changed. Now we value time and money differently. We also try to do everything differently. Our tastes have changed too, and we have started to devote more time to certain activities. We have changed our leisure time. We have redefined our priorities; and although the course of our lives has remained the same, we see the world differently. Now I react differently when I listen to the news. Our interests have changed too.

In my opinion, the most difficult thing is to swim against the current by yourself. I dream of a community of preppers, which exist in certain US states. It seems to me that it is easier as part of a group. Now we are getting the impression that we still have to learn everything, and that our whole lives won't be long enough to do it, because we are continuing to exist in the modern world, with all of its demands. It is very difficult to organize alone, to learn alone.

It is also very difficult to find enough time to do everything that we want, to learn what is interesting.

There is also a problem with money. Everyone wants there to be more of it, in order for the preparations to move along faster. But in the end we are forced to find a different way out of the situation.

As far as how other people see us... In the beginning it wasn't easy. But when you start to talk about it, it gets easier. I also think that the uncertainty that has gripped the world opens up a path toward dialogue. People become convinced that there is a certain amount of sense in it. Unfortunately, only a few people begin to act. The majority prefer to hope that nothing will happen, or think that they will have time. People react in different ways. I would like to have the possibility of speaking about this more freely, but some people are very afraid and prefer to avoid conversations on this subject or even mention it in passing. Others listen and smile, and don't believe any of it. But I have come to terms with this. Those around us are by now used to the fact that we are going against the current; for example, that we home-school our children.

In order to defend our children, we could resort to weapons, but we hope that we won't have to. Or that we will only do so in an extreme situation. We prefer to use our weapons to hunt. But the fact that we live in a remote village forces us to take certain measures to defend ourselves. It would be easy to completely cut us off from the outside world by blocking two or three roads. And then we, together with the thousand residents of the village, would be forced to find a way out of the situation on our own. I believe that security is directly connected with common sense, neighborliness and respect for social values.

I don't think that my preparation changes anything fundamental in my relationship with my children. Of course, we are bringing up our children in such a way that they understand what is happening. As I already said, we have changed our leisure, and have developed new pursuits. But since we homeschool our children, they do not feel any external pressure on themselves and share our strivings in the most natural way possible. I consider this a great success.

What can you do when you find yourself in a situation and can't find a way out on your own, being dependent on the system? To be autonomous means, in a certain sense, to be free. In addition I, as a woman, feel a huge need to defend my family. I also realize that the people of my generation are gradually returning to their roots, even if they are driven by different motivations or pursue different goals.

I recommend that women who are interested in preparing and reading these lines start by gathering information and becoming convinced of the necessity to make changes, because this will make it easier not to fall into despair and give up. This also makes it easier to talk to those near to us. I think that we need to move forward in small steps, without attempting too much at once. This is impossible to achieve in a short period of time. Even if you will be only 5 percent prepared, this is still better than nothing. And so, to move forward, one step after another, you have to create an overall plan and to carry it out gradually. When you look back, you see that, imperceptibly, you have covered great distance.

I also recommend that women think rationally without allowing themselves to be ruled by fear. The more active you are, the easier it is to prepare. Of course, it is very important to be armed with good information. But it is very dangerous to remain at the level of theoretical knowledge, forgetting that activity is much more important. I also recommend turning preparation into an exciting adventure, one in which children will participate with pleasure. How pleasant it is to learn about your environment, to devote your activities to survival, to lay in supplies of food and so on... You become a sort of pioneer, in search of lost knowledge. Nobody is traumatized by this; quite the opposite, it becomes a wonderful family adventure. Discuss it with your entire families.

My advice for men is as follows. Try to combine your way of thinking with your wife's way of thinking. Forget about the "Rambo" aspect and try to see the problem from a woman's point of view. And they you will have a greater chance of involving your wives in your activities. We, women, are interested in everything that has to do with everyday living, with practical things, with applying our knowledge to family life. Good luck!

Aviva

"Become masters of your fate!"

I am 42 years old, married, mother of four-year-old twins. I am head of a company that offers information services, which I created in 2005 and which now employs 60 people. I live near the town Petakh-Tikhva, to the north of Tel-Aviv, in Israel.

In my country we are all a little bit paranoid when talking about the future. My grandmothers and grandfathers fled from Hungary and Rumania in 1945 after Nazi persecutions, and my parents met in Galilee, on a kibbutz. It is possible to say that the urge to survive is in my blood! But I must admit that in spite of all the wars we survived when I was still small (the Yom-Kippur war, the war in Lebanon, two intifadas, the Persian Gulf war, bombardment by Iraqi Scud rockets, another war in Lebanon) I only thought about being ready to go into the cellar with my family in case of bombings. It was enough for me to have a bag with a minimal kit to leave the house in case it became necessary, a gas mask in case of a chemical attack and weapons to defend the house... When I worked with Piero San Giorgio, one evening we started to discuss his plan for transforming life. When he told me that he is leaving a well-paying job in order to settle on a farm, I told myself that it is essential for me to think about this seriously. Later on I "hired" him as a consultant, so that he could help me equip our small farm.

Yes, I am afraid that future years will be difficult for everyone, that the economy will be falling apart and becoming worse and worse. And I am heading up a small company, and people are counting on me, and I won't leave them in the lurch, them or their families. At the present moment things aren't going too badly, knock on wood.

We live in a small house with a large garden. We got lucky, I and my husband (who also works in information technology): we bought this house before the prices went up because of land speculation. We didn't have to get a mortgage and could invest all of our earnings in equipping the house as a small farm. We have a kitchen garden, chickens, date palms, orange trees—and this provides us not just with fruits and vegetables, but gives us joy because of its beauty.

Our main problem is water. Essentially, it only rains in the winter, and so we installed two large cisterns for collecting rainwater. Near the house there is an old well, dug in the 1960s, but it no longer reaches the water table, which dropped because of intensive agriculture. Everybody is afraid that if things go badly the public services will not be able to continuously provide water. And so we bought Berkey[123] water filters, which we will be able to use to purify rainwater. We installed a solar water heater, and this year we are planning to install a photogalvanic module for producing a small quantity of energy. All of these mechanisms work on solar panels. This makes us autonomous in case of blackouts.

As far as defense, this is all obvious. In addition to sporadic burglaries, we are mainly afraid of war. I am a patriot, I have served in the army,[124] but I am a liberal and active in the move-

---

123 See www.bigberkeywaterfilters.com.
124 Israel has mandatory military service, with the minimal length of service 3 years for men and 22 months for women.

214

ment "Peace Now."[125] I am unhappy with the politics of our ever-changing governments, which do not want to entirely give back the occupied territories to the Palestinians, or to recognize all of the settlements there as illegal. If you don't consider geopolitics and aren't very well informed, then it is impossible to correctly predict my country's future. In a word, if problems arise, they will be very serious. Consequently, it is essential to calculate how much time my country can last without engaging in negotiations. The more time passes, the clearer it becomes that these discussions will not be to our advantage. This means that we have to prepare. My husband and I have completed military service, we have weapons at home (two old but still good rifles and revolvers, and that's not that little) and we know how to use them. In contrast to many rich people, who leave the country or buy houses in Latin America, preparing to flee, my husband and I have decided to stay here. We were born here. Our children were born here. This is our country.

Just as many other local residents, we have some fuel in jerrycans, in case of shortages. But a fuel shortage would be a huge problem, because the country is very dependent on road transport and cars.

125 "Shalom Ashkhav" is an Israeli nonparlamentary movement created in 1978 by 300 officers of the reserve. It is independent of political parties, and is left of center. Its goal is to "convince public opinion and Israeli government in the possibility and necessity to reach a just and stable peace through negotiations based on the principle "Two peoples —two states," and reaching peace between Israel and a future Palestinian state, as well as neighboring Arab countries." This movement lobbies for the recognition of the Palestinian state, even though it considers itself Zionist.

Everybody thinks that Israeli women are very independent and liberated, but this is not really so. Many women are convinced that everything should be done by men. In our family we distribute purchases, but on weekends we work in the garden together. In the final analysis, preparation, especially together with neighborhood committees which gather regularly to discuss the necessary actions in case of war, a terrorist attack or other catastrophes, allows us to strengthen social connections. If our house burned down, the neighbors would take us in. And we would do the same.

I want to advise women who will be reading your book to think independently and not allow themselves to be influenced by archaic superstitions... Become masters of your destiny!

As far as the men, I would like to tell them that we love you as husbands and defenders. But please don't think that we don't know how to do anything! We can do everything just as well as you! And that includes defending our family.

Muriel

"A woman has to be independent, brave, athletic, shrewd, charismatic, fore-sighted."

My name is Muriel, I am 40 and I have no children. I have a degree in physical education (UFRSTPS), a Masters in sports management and the title of Master of Sports. In 2004, before I received this title, I was accepted to serve in the municipal police. In January of 2005 I started working in the municipal police in Montpelier.

Since then I have enrolled in a college, and I practice sports a lot. I have been boxing for 12 years. I also teach French boxing (Savat) and American kickboxing (full-contact). I stopped taking part in competitions and now practice once a week. I box and practice moves used by the police, because of my service in Montpelier's night brigade for three years now.

In a word, I am a man by calling.

If a woman works, the she is independent on every level. Today it is possible to find women in virtually every profession, at all levels of the social ladder, even though they do not always receive the same pay as men. Today more and more women are doing manual labor and participate in men's types of sports. Possibly because they live alone, or for the sake of saving money, or as a hobby, many women—more and more every day—are preparing and learning martial arts in order to defend themselves. This is exactly the tendency I have noticed working in clubs.

In my opinion it is very important that women prepare for life's difficulties, no matter how serious. In the current circumstances everything is becoming serious. During crisis the frequency of attacks with the use of violence increases along with rapes and thefts. And let's not forget about natural disasters. War and terrorism are knocking at our door.

Taking into account the state of today's world, a woman has to be independent, brave, athletic, shrewd, charismatic and foresighted.

Unfortunately, as far as I can see, few women are concerned with their own security and the safety of their families! But I get the impression that this situation is changing. I can observe this when visiting martial arts clubs, which are attended by more and more women every year. In any case, I would like to remind all the women who are preparing of a saying by Emperor Marcus Aurelius: "Develop your independence every moment—with good will, simplicity and humility."

Florentine

> "In the village, the old-timers never felt a lack of food."

I am 45 years old, unmarried, no children. I live in Romania, in Bucharest, where I am the head of the local office (1,000 employees) of a multinational company that handles road transport logistics.

Five or six years ago I started thinking about what would happen if companies such as the one that employs me will become unable to function, either because of an economic crisis, or because of a natural disaster, or because of lack of fuel. In such cases the large cities in my country will stop being supplied.

I started by renting out my apartment, which is located in the center of the city, and bought another apartment outside of town, in Otopeni, on the road to Ploiești, which is a town that has oil wells and refineries. There I am not far from my job, or from a zone that will undoubtedly be better defended and better supplied (highway, airport, military base). The only detraction is that it is close to shopping centers and a gigantic Ikea, which in a crisis will either become a target for looters, or will be abandoned.

In my new apartment, which is located in a leafy suburb, I started to make minimal stockpiles of food and water. I renew them based on the principle of first-in, first-out. I have enough supplies to last me a month. Perhaps I will increase them in the future. I have a tiny garden on the territory of the building where my apartment is located. There I have started growing potatoes and other vegetables. On advice of one of my friends I planted sunchokes on an empty lot behind the airport, not far from my house. It seems that this plant, which has edible tubers, is quick to spread. It will be interesting to see if anything comes of this.

I also learned to defend myself, having completed a self-defense course, and have joined a marksmanship club. I hope that I will soon receive a permit to buy firearms, since our laws about gun ownership are very strict. To start with I chose a 9mm pistol. Later I will probably buy a shotgun.

The biggest risk for me is this. If such a large city as Bucharest will suddenly stop being supplied and will experience shortages of everything, then I am afraid that many people with bad intentions will come to our little corner. And so I worked out a simple evacuation plan, which will allow me to reach my parents' house, which is near the small town of Baia Mare, in the north of the country. If I have a full tank of gas I shouldn't have a problem. This is an agricultural region, with small traditional homesteads that grow vegetables, breed pigs and so on. In the village the old-timers never experienced a lack of food—neither during the war, nor under socialism, no during the deep economic crisis during the transitional period in the 1990s.

Since I live alone, I can rely only on myself and my family (I have a sister who lives in my home town, and I often go to visit her). I try to have good relations with my neighbors who, it would seem, approve of my actions. There is an old tradition here to look out for each other and to defend against small thefts and burglaries committed by... how should I say?... by the representatives of one of our national minorities, many of whom have left for France.[126] In a word, we remain a serious people that is quick to sort things out. The only unfortunate thing is that the men here are such chauvinists.

---

126 These are most likely the Roma, a.k.a. the Gypsies.

Julianne

"My children love our lifestyle."

I am 36 years old. I come from a family of 9 with two younger sisters and four younger brothers. I am a permaculture sustainable farmer and YouTuber – my channel is "Dirtpatcheaven." My family has always been prepared. We live in Idaho, in rough country and when nature takes over and gets violent we have always had supplies on hand to help us survive and thrive. When I was five we lived in Wyoming and a snowstorm buried our town so that you could walk over the top and not see roofs or chimneys. We were just fine because my dad had emergency heaters, food, and shovels in the house and he dug us out and we were warm and safe inside. I still remember the smell of the kerosene stove that kept us warm.

I believe that environmental toxins are our most pressing danger. We have soiled our own nest and now have nowhere clean to run to. This is why I am a farmer, we have to fix our soil and protect our families rather than waiting for government or someone else to come and do it.

I am always independent and prepared. I was raised this way and it has been a huge...an enormous blessing to our family. When my husband got hurt and couldn't work we didn't have to go on food stamp or any other kind of government or family assistance. We had food storage, we had our livestock that fed us, and we had paid our mortgage forward so that for six months we had no bills. We actually lived a little better while my husband was out of work because he didn't have to spend gas and lunches to get to work and back. I have a small business but all of the money from that went back into the farm, none of it had to go toward bills.

I don't find preparedness stressful, I would find not prepping to be very stressful. I am able to claim other peoples' unwanted objects and use or sell them. We eat from our own land. We don't use credit unless it is for a very short period of time in an emergency and then we pay it off very quickly. Our only debt is our small mortgage and we are paying it off as fast as we can. To me it means freedom.

I find the time to prepare by having good skills and constantly educating myself. I was raised to be prepared so I don't know any other way to live. I cook from scratch, I sew, I garden...what other way is there to be?

My priority in independence is food. If you don't have good food you don't have good health. Our animals keep us so healthy that we don't need a dentist, we don't have cavities while drinking raw goats milk. We research health principles and live by them most of the time so that very rarely do we need a doctor. When we do need a doctor we go to one that does not believe in insurance. We pay cash and it costs $20, and he is a real doctor, he just wants people to be healthy and finds that he makes enough money without messing with insurance.

My most important skill is using my brain. I am always strategizing. If I see a raw material I think through how to use it to it's best advantage or sell it. How can I make this faster? How can I make it cheaper? How can I....? I am always educating myself.

We buy everything in bulk. We buy almost nothing in retail. We buy 20-50 lb. bags of dry goods and put it second hand buckets from the bakery. We buy hay for our animals for the whole winter rather than for a month. We buy grain for our chickens from a feed mill rather than a hobby farm store. It saves us thousands of dollars a year. We eat out of our food storage rather than saving it for 30 years. If food storage goes bad we cook it and feed it to the pigs or chickens over the winter. Then we also end up with pork and chicken in the freezer. We only use cash and have an envelope system that pays the bills. If we don't need the money for the bill it stays there and builds up like a savings account. If a commodity we need goes on sale we have months worth of money that allows us to buy a ton of grain at a great price and all we have to do is store it until we need it.

I have never lived any other way. My mother and father raised me this way and when people see what I am doing they are amazed but it is all about education.

I don't have a lot of social pressure. Before I started my YouTube channel I felt lonely because the women around me weren't working the way I was and didn't understand why I didn't wear fancy clothes and look nice as a farmer. Now that I am on YouTube other women have found me that do the same things and I have community.

Before I started making money at what I do my family was worried about how hard i was working and counseled me to stop. As I learned to market my skills online my family is now very excited and supportive of what I am doing.

I believe that in an extreme situation having skills will be your best protection. We have taken classes and have tools that allow us to protect ourselves from violence but I think it would really depend on the situation. What is the danger? Is it human or nature or chemical? In each situation your approach would be different. I cannot look to far in the future on this question. If I get too bogged down by fear and speculation I can't effectively take care of my family in the now.

My children love our lifestyle. The one thing that we are working to improve right now is doing more fun activities away from our home. Finding inexpensive activities that are still helping our objective are the best. We can take our bikes into town on our truck and then strengthen ourselves and our kids with a bike ride while we go garage sale shopping for supplies for our farm products store. We also like to go on little road trips to see other farmers and learn new skills. That is very important, to find ways to let your children play and socialize and not always be talking about preparedness. Our girls do all of the small animal chores and much of the cooking. They are paid for this work so that they have money to pay for their own clothes and tools. We also homeschool so we are very aware of our need to not raise our children isolated and in fear.

As for advice? I would say start cooking from scratch. Once you have that down educate yourself about tools that will help you to start cooking from scratch from bulk. Your food supply is so important that it is your first priority and if you are spending too much money on retail groceries you have no money to invest in preparedness!

To the men I would say give your wife the preparedness activities that she loves and feels are important. Don't dump on her something you don't want to do. Fitting people into the activities and skills they already have is the easiest way to prep.

Jessica

"Behind every great man there is always a great woman."

My name is Jessica, I am 29 years old, I am married and have a child. I am a full-time homemaker and mother. We live in the province of Novara, in Italy. I started "prepping" more seriously since I became a mother in 2015. I knew about it before, because my husband is part of a group of Italian preppers, but I did not consider it too important. At first, I thought it was some sort of football club! One time, while sharing a pizza with some members of my husband's group, they exclaimed, ironically: "OK, you can join, provided you don't do drugs!" But when I saw that this group was about more than just picnics and barbecues, I upgraded my opinion of it, and in 2016 I joined it.

The trigger, as I said, was the birth of my baby, and my predictable decision to leave work to look after it. That's when I realized what it means to stock up, to prepare things at home, and how to handle difficult crisis situations.

Our first challenge was economic, figuring out how to make ends meet for three people plus a dog on just one salary. This proved to be easier than we expected, because we were able to resurrect the old techniques learned from our grandparents: growing and preserving our own food. Another major risk definitely has to do with the economic crisis we are already facing, which I don't think will be over any time soon. So we have to prepare to make do without various products and services, which we will surely miss, for example, if running water is not available anymore. As far as the future, I see the financial crisis as a big problem, and I can't deny the possibility that there will be terrorist attacks, and the possible imposition of a martial law.

I don't have a set time that I devote to preparing, because preparing is a daily activity. I wake up in the morning and I devote myself to the daily shopping, house-cleaning, and especially to teaching our son to learn to deal with the worst situations, although for now he is still too young to understand. But I am already playing with him instead of watching TV, feeding him food that we can prepare ourselves, showing him how important it is to properly prepare food at home, including making preserves and canning, which, among other things, I consider really fun and relaxing. I also explore natural cleaning methods, such as using baking soda, which I think is a godsend, work in the orchard, learn crafts that are disappearing, such as sewing, knitting and so on. I take courses on how to deal with certain situations, first aid, self-defense, etc. With regard to time, we try to involve the entire family, thus making it a family business, and I can say that this works: our budget works because of economizing and doing some work at home.

For us, the priority in the process of gaining our independence is energy. I consider it a priority, but since for now we are living in condominium, it is a bit of a utopia. But we are optimistic that in the future we will be able to buy a small house with an adjoining plot of land and to grow what we need, perhaps even keep some livestock.

There are skills that are necessary to avoid having to call specialists: electricians, plumbers, mechanics, etc. We are still buying DIY books, so that we at least have the theoretical knowledge that we can later put into practice.

Considering that only my husband works and for now I am collecting unemployment, our investments are small but clever and targeted to have a clear economic benefit, or generate some income that allows us to help make ends meet and move forward. We bought a semiprofessional sewing machine to do tailoring, and also to make backpacks and fanny packs for members of the prepper group. My husband is getting involved in learning various skills such as metal working, carpentry, electronics, leather processing, so that we have something to fall back on if something goes wrong.

As for making a stockpile, fortunately we have a fairly large cellar, and are able to store food supplies and materials for cleaning and hygiene which we buy in bulk when there is a mega-offer at the supermarket. As of today we can remain autonomous of one year. We take great care to rotate stocks to avoid costly losses. As for the division of labor, this is very simple: all the jobs for which you need physical strength are done by my husband, while I take care of the home and the child care, of course, and also work to make ends meet. When my husband a bit of free time he spends time with our baby and gives me a hand with the housework.

Initially it was not easy for me to take to this new way of life, but in a short time I realized that it is actually easier than expected. We have never been filthy rich, but now I realize that I'm much healthier, and we can now afford some luxury every now and again, more often than before. But of course such luxuries are always geared toward further preparation, such as a vacation in an adventure park, or even camping. The hardest part was learning how to do things for the house—not

228

so much for my husband, who has always done it and has a passion for these things. But for me it was hard, learning to do canning (because before it was my husband who did the cooking), and to do things without various products and services, which we actually don't need.

How do other people see us? I'll be honest, they envy us, whenever they have a problem and have call a specialist, or call me and my husband, and we help them without asking anything in return. Here we have an advantage, because they always ask how much the job costs, but we don't charge for our time, especially if it's for close friends and family. Instead, we find ourselves at home with something useful—food especially. One episode I remember is when my husband repaired a car for some dear friends, and they thanked him by giving us a 9 kg ham. Then one time my wonderful neighbor (I say "wonderful" because she is a lovely person), when she had a problem with her computer, she called my husband, who obviously did not ask her for money. And then the very next day she brought us a box with 10 kg of brown sugar, fresh eggs, preserves, honey and more.

In case of a serious emergency, we prepare to deal with it the only way possible. In case of serious sociopolitical or environmental problems, we will rely on the people who are closest to us: friends and relatives.

As for my son, it is still a bit soon to involve him, because he is less than two years old. But my initial impression is that my baby responds well to all sorts of stimuli, and I can see that he learns very quickly. I will be able to tell you more in a few years.

As a woman, I am thoroughly convinced that it is important to work toward independence and autonomy, because I believe that this is the best solution, given how things are going in this world.

To a friend who would like to get started on the project of becoming independent, my advice is to read up on as things as possible, using books and the internet, but it is even better if you already know someone who practices this lifestyle.

My message to the men who will be reading this book is this: trust your women, and if you speak to them about prepar-ing, do so gently, and remember that behind every great man there is a great woman.

Rebecca

"I advise you to view the person beside
you as a valuable ally."

My name is Rebecca, I am 33 years old and I live in Tuscany.
I live with my husband, a cat and two parrots. Currently we do
not have any children, by choice.

I am licensed as a surveyor. I studied Biology at the University of Pisa, and then ended up becoming an artist, doing jewelry, decoration and furniture detailing. For a year now I have
been taking part in the world of Comics as an exhibitor. In December I was joined by my husband, because the company
where he worked had closed. For many people this would have
been a catastrophe, because we don't have a stable income, but
we were prepared for this sort of emergency.

When did I started thinking outside the box that is the modern world? My maternal grandfather had been an Alpine
"white feather" (the famous Italian mountain troops) and I often went to meetings with him and my grandmother, who
were still marked by their memories of the Second World War.

I still remember the food stockpiles, especially of sugar,
which they used to keep in the pantry, because you just never
know when something unexpected might hit you. My grandmother had really missed the sugar.

One afternoon I was at the ophthalmologist's with my husband (we were still engaged at the time) and we were both
reading an article in the National Geographic on solar flares
and how they could bring the present civilization back to the
days before the discovery of electricity. Unfortunately, we are

no longer able to survive without the electric grid, especially in large cities, because even the water that flows from the taps is in most cases powered by an electric pump.

We exchanged a look of understanding, and we knew that we had to at least try to prepare for this possibility. And so we began to cultivate the soil that was available to us, and we began to stockpile food.

In time we began to realize that it was not just the sun that could be a hindrance to the homeostasis of our life, but that so could many other events. Our climate is changing and the country in which we live is very fragile. It doesn't take a catastrophic event, such as a war, for us to be in danger; just a landslide, a flood or a hurricane, which have happened in these parts in recent years, could leave us isolated for days or weeks.

The historical period in which we live is very uncertain, the crisis has affected many sectors of the economy and many businesses have closed, causing job losses for many workers. Unfortunately, many were unable to survive in this situation, and have taken their lives.

The world in which we live is one of of constant daily conflicts, and history teaches us that often the quickest way to resolve an economic crisis is to start a war.

I have not set a fixed a time for preparing for possible events, since I have made it part of my lifestyle, and don't stress out over it. Our budget remains quite reasonable, because I take advantage of discounts and coupons to stock up. I get many products straight from the earth, from what I gather seasonally. My biggest investment is in knowledge and in continuous curiosity, in figuring out which plants are not only edible, which is something many people already know, but which can be used for phytotherapy, because in case of an EMP there will be no more drug companies to supply us with drugs.

Over the years I have studied the techniques our ancestors had used for sustaining themselves, such as how to make soap from ash, cheese, yogurt, wild yeast, etc.

I organize the food stockpile in convenient boxes, sorted by type and expiration date. They are rotated on a monthly basis, in order to use up those with the earliest expiration date, and what was the last to be purchased will be what the last to be consumed.

I buy fresh foods once or twice a week.

The only inconvenience is in having to organize everything in a limited space of 48 square meters, since we also have our laboratory at home.

Over the course of the last years we have decided to give ourselves different options in case of a possible event, and we are also focusing on organizing a second place up in the hills that is more isolated, in order to have a totally self-sufficient place.

We started to learn bushcraft and wilderness survival techniques. So we tried to split up the work. I take care of organizing, cataloging, cultivating, storing, cooking and canning, because they are all things I am good at, while he is responsible for managing and updating the emergency kit for both of us and helps me to organize alternative plans.

My life has changed in that I have started to feel more secure. I don't find this lifestyle tiring, because I live in harmony and awareness. I live like all other women, I work, I run the the house, I see friends and go shopping. Only instead of going to the gym to breathe other people's carbon dioxide, I prefer to walk in the woods and the fields, breathing oxygen while gathering something for dinner. Instead of lifting weights I dig up the earth. Instead of watching "Friends" I'd rather watch "Out of this World" on Sky Network.

My family has learned to accept my new way of thinking and living, and they are often intrigued by what we do, and even though they will never admit it, they also tend to stock up, as the older generations had done, that we have lost because of affluence.

Ten years ago my friends could not understand why we were doing this, and we were often laughed at. Over the years some of them have become more mature, and although they do not share our choice, they have come to respect it. I live in a resort town full of with nightclubs and VIPs, where having fun is almost mandatory. Honestly, I've always felt like a fish out of water, because I have never been drawn to the nightlife. I tread lightly when speaking of our choice, and listen carefully, to see if they seem reluctant, in which case I do not insist. Often, however, I realize that so many people are interested, perhaps thanks to the television programs that have appeared in recent years, which have approached this topic in a way that appeals to common people.

I think that today's society wants to make us women less and less free, contrary to what they would like us to believe. The continuous hammering on television at the female stereotype, in which beauty is the only thing that matters, has made us increasingly enslaved by a lifestyle that does not represent us.

I often talk about bags and shoes with my girlfriends like everyone else, but unfortunately some of them stop there. Fortunately, more often than you'd think, they are driven by curiosity and love of their family to better understand how to prepare for a possible emergency.

I think that as a woman I feel lucky, because I have a husband and a family, and they have never tried to restrict my options because of who I am, supporting me no matter what choices I made, even if they were quite bizarre.

My husband, on his own initiative, is learning to handle various household tasks, so that we can both be self-sufficient.

I think that we shouldn't underestimate the skills that women have. We should not be the ones who just cook and clean for everyone, but we should also be able to make a real contribution to emergency management. Over the years I gained confidence that I didn't think I had. I have learned a lot about bladed weapons, not to mention self-defense techniques. The person you live with should be a real ally, some you trust and with whom you have a special feeling of solidarity.

My personal recommendation is that every woman should make the choice for greater self-sufficiency and, above all, for greater awareness. It is not wrong to go back to the old ways of our forebears. We have gone too far in a world that goes too fast, and instead of gaining ground, we have lost health, skills and knowledge. We have entrusted our lives and our families to a false affluence, where material possessions have replaced feelings.

You do not need to have thousands of euros to get started. You can do a little at a time. You have to be curious, read a lot, inquire. You can find good ideas on the internet and many books. You don't need to immediately plant hectares of land, you can start with some flower pots. The important thing is to do it with enthusiasm and to never give up.

To the men who will read this book, I would like to suggest that they look at the person who is next to them as a valuable ally. The right approach is to start on this path together, to avoid constantly talking about weapons and war, because this will inhibit us from the beginning. We women are much more likely to care about the management and organization of the stockpiles and of the house. I advise you to take these steps to - gether in the most natural and fun way possible, being equally open to new ideas.

In Conclusion:
The Ball is In Your Court

"It does not behoove you to cry and stomp your feet like a woman at the moment when you lose that which you did not succeed in defending like a man because had neither enough willpower nor enough courage."
—Aisha al-Khorr, addressing her son Boabdil, the last Moorish emir of Granada (1492)

"If there is no pressure, there are no diamonds."
—Mary Case, American playwright (1960-2002)

"The adventure itself is worthy of interest."
—Amelia Earhart, aviation pioneer (1897-1937)

The century between 1914 and 2014, with its economic growth and social accomplishments, made possible thanks to plentiful natural resources and technological progress, was "women's century."

My grandmother Margarita would, no doubt, agree with me!

That century, insignificant on the scale of our long history, represents the sum of progressive achievements as sudden as they are impressive. None of our ancestors, not even those who, like Jules Verne,[127] were endowed with a brave imagination, could have even thought of such progress, or of the speed with which it burst into our everyday life.

But the modern world has its dark side: the crawling, noisy, polluting humanity; the global, interconnected and vulnerable economy; social progress that forgot what is reasonable, good and eternal; scientific and technological research, sometimes very promising, but often locked into fruitless narcissism...

Even if we are cognizant of these problems—thanks to our education or to what we see and read in mass media, or because of personal intuition—nevertheless the realities of our modernity, its global nature, its vulnerability, its interconnectedness and complex mechanisms remain difficult to grasp in all of their aspects, because we are too busy to hold a hand on its pulse.

And we continue to trust, to delegate our future and our security to existing systems and authorities.

Of course, it is sometimes difficult to hear and agree with a message that may elicit anxiety and alarm, especially if it

127 Jules Verne (1828-1905) was a writer whose work had a profound influence on the genre of science-fiction.

touches upon the very foundations of our life. In encountering this inescapable reality many of us—men and women, young and old, poor and rich—choose to do nothing, perpetuating not just a culture of excessive dependence and submission, but also a certain collective inertia in the face of crises and emergency situations, be they large or small, personal or global.

Now you realize that such crises can be traffic accidents, burglaries, water and electricity outages, a fire in your home,[128] loss of employment, death of one of the people close to you, violent attack when you exit a shop or the subway, rape, unrest, natural disaster, terrorist attack, food shortage, sudden bout of inflation, epidemic, systemic collapse of the entire economy[129] and the consequences of serious geopolitical crises.[130]

For women these crisis situations carry a high risks of suffering abuse stemming from the possibility of sharp and sudden limitations placed on their freedom and independence. If in our days the stability of the world allows us to support social progress and defend the rights won by and for women, what will become of these achievements if tomorrow this stability comes under threat, becomes shaky or disappears?

It would be useful to analyze a few of the recent crises:

How were women treated inside the New Orleans Superdome during hurricane Katrina?

---

128 In France a house fire erupts every two minutes.
129 As happened in Germany in the 1920s, in the former Soviet Union, former Yugoslavia and Argentina in the 1990s, in Zimbabwe in 2000s and so on.
130 Such as wars, including civil wars.

How did the women of Sarajevo survive during the hight of the war in the Balkans... and how are they surviving today in Iraq or Syria?

How did women fare under the conditions of economic collapse in the former Soviet Union, Argentina, Zimbabwe... and now in Greece, Spain or in the tent cities inhabited by the homeless in the United States?

Foresightedness demands some sort of attempt to achieve a modicum of stability, in order to mitigate the risks associated with crises, no matter what their nature.

In other words, it means acquiring, on our level and using a variety of strategies, the means of upholding the norm, in the face of external coercion, and the ability to control our wellbeing.

Everything depends on the choices and methods of our actions.

Foresightedness was the main determinant of our species' survival during 99.9 percent of its existence on the this planet. But today it is too often understood and perceived—thanks to the efforts of mass media and television—as something aberrant, as exalted pessimism, as an attack of acute paranoia or as the product of anxious fantasies.

The thing is, the majority of us are convinced that we are completely protected from any emergency, any crisis. We prefer to follow one of the most feckless forms of behavior: we do nothing.

This passivity is the result of a systematic rejection of reality, if not to say a fatalism, which can be compared to the thoughtless gaze of a rabbit that is looking into the headlights of a car that is about to crush it, and it is always justified using the same set of arguments:

This only happens to others!

This is my husband's concern!

No catastrophe can happen here; we live in a developed country, and a way can always be found out of any situation!

Neighbors, firemen, police, army or the government will come to my aid!

As a woman, I don't want to do anything...

Today as never before it is becoming risky to play the role of a passive spectator. This risk is reflected in the ever-increasing vulnerability of our contemporary world, and in our own helplessness and lack of coordination. But we are too myopic to be able to see that.

If we discard this refusal to accept reality, then our independence, our level of autonomy and our stability are the only real constructs capable of creating a livable space for us, in which we will be the true masters of our fate.

But, in the end, will we really be masters of our fate if tomorrow water stops flowing from the taps? If tomorrow, because of 1000 percent inflation, food prices suddenly increase, as happened in Argentina in 1998-2002? If tomorrow the cost of electricity goes up 1000 percent, or if it is shut off and our refrigerators, central heating and health care system stop working? What if tomorrow a liter of gasoline costs 10 euro?

If any of this happens... we will be left only with that which nobody and nothing can take away from us: our knowledge, our skills, our strong ties within the family and within society. In the final account, to develop them is the only true means we can resort to, in order to try to guarantee our stability, our independence, our freedom.

This approach is by no means based on fear. Quite the opposite: it is based on knowledge and actions; it is supported also by the undeniable facts that nobody in the world loves your children as you do, that nobody in the world feels your need for security and stability as you do, that nobody in the world will be able to defend your family as well as you can, that nobody in the world can value your freedom and independence as you.

The examples of the women who became the stars of this book show that nobody else in the world except you will concern themselves with your physical and psychological health and well-being or that of the people you love.

In the final analysis, you will gain a life that is filled with greater meaning, greater reality and—why not?—with greater happiness.

Conclusion to the Italian Edition

> "God mocks those who deplore the effects of causes they cherish."
> —Jacques-Bénigne Bossuet – French bishop, 1627-1704

This book speaks of women, and lets some of them have the word.

In conclusion, allow me me to offer a man's advice for women to survive economic collapse.

I wrote this book before the events in Cologne.[131] Before there exploded the epidemic of sexual assault and rape committed by foreign populations in Europe.[132] These events,

---

131 This is in reference to the sexual assaults and rapes perpetrated against German women in Cologne on December 31, 2015.

132 Allowing into a pacifist and guilt-ridden Europe, with a population that has an average IQ of 100, and with an economy that is based on knowledge and services, populations with an average IQ of 70-80, that are 40 percent illiterate in their native language, and of which 85 percent are sexually

which are only in their early stages, showed many women the kinds of risks they face in a society where their protection was delegated to the State and where the men no longer protect them.

And yet we want to protect you!

In part it's because that's our instinct. Biologically, men are programmed to protect their mothers, sisters, daughters, and women in general that belong to their own cultural, ethnic or national group, because they bear their offspring and therefore assure the passage of their genes. Among themselves, men compete for the highest possible social status in order to gain access to the most attractive women (young, beautiful and fertile) with whom they are ready to share the resources they acquire through their work and ambition.

In part it is because we appreciate you as our natural and indispensable complements and companions in life: we need you to establish a healthy and balanced family, so that we may share in the joys as well as the difficulties of life, compensate for each other's faults, and have you encourage us and push us to become better.

But that was before.

Since then, feminism pushed women to become equal to men, to work, to be independent, and to no longer need them. The welfare state even allows women who lack resources to "make mistakes" in their choice of men and to raise children alone or with men who are too fickle to stay. Sure of their rights, and the financial support that results from with any divorce or paternity claim, women can also afford to abuse their

---

frustrated young men from a traditionally violent culture... what could possibly go wrong?

men, verbally and physically, and push them out of the relationship.

Very well...

But then men no longer see it as advantageous to share the
resources they acquire, and have no ambitions beyond satisfying their narcissistic sexuality and their consumerist ego. They
no longer need to do any more than give empty promises,
which the women—being in fierce competition with each
other—prefer to believe. Many of these women then complain
of being unable to find a partner in life who would devote himself to raising her children. Meanwhile, a man can act like a
teenager half his life, pursue a career, and then, when he is 40
or 50 and has the financial means, have children with a
younger woman.

For many women, their careers are often reduced to the
function of a glorified secretary or a public relations officer,
obliged to spend their income on the tinsel and trinkets of
fashion that are necessary to remain in competition with other
women. The option of starting a family, more and more often
as a single mother, is a very difficult one. Thus, many women
choose not to have children[133] and finish their lives alone and
sad, with a pet for company, and with memories of a sex life,
certainly varied but emotionally frustrating, as their only compensation. They might also have some gold-plated pens com-

---

133 The fertility rate in Italy in 2015 was 1.38, whereas, for example, in the
Niger its 7.19, 5.32 in Nigeria, 4.26 in Iraq... If you don't have children, then
someone else will. This someone else will often come either from parasitic
cultures, or from ones that have never developed the organizational ability
to build or maintain a complex civilization, or from ones that hold totalitarian beliefs and are nihilistic and violent.

memorating their years of loyal service to some business that has since disappeared. Some deal!

And the worst case scenario is that, absent loving children, once the economic crisis destroys pensions and social benefits, they will have no one to care for them. As for those who did have children, but had them brought up by nannies, daycare centers and the school system—because they were too preoc-cupied with pleasing their employer, or with pursuing their ambition, to devote themselves to their children, to teach them and to bring them up as moral individuals—what is there to ensure that emotional ties are sufficiently strong for their children to do anything other than pack them off to a nursing home or a home for the elderly?

I do not speak of this to be flippant, or out of spite, but be-cause this is the reality.

The feminists never miss a chance to criticize, one more time, the sort of society they like to call "patriarchal" (all the while the would-be "patriarchs" are disappearing, being criti-cized and financially taxed from all sides) or "macho" (all the while men are being ridiculed and shown as weak and submis-sive in numerous films and television series). Really? But where are all the feminists when women are being assaulted?

Following the rapes in Cologne and other European cities, their reaction could be summed up as "all men are rapists." All of them? And yet 100 percent of the more than a thousand sex-ual assaults committed that night were committed by immi-grants from Afghanistan, the Middle East or North Africa. In Sweden, the second-rapiest country in the world (after Lesotho) 100 percent of rapes are committed by non-Euro-peans. That's 100 percent; not 50 percent, not 80 percent, 100 percent!

No, the feminists are not protecting women. They do not want equality. They want to assure the dominance of a certain group of women over all other people—men and women. They want more money from the state in the form of academic positions and grants to associations. Deep down, they are crusaders, driven by their hate of men—specifically, of white men.

Alas, the problem is that when we men are made to feel guilty and are punished for acting as men and as protectors of women by a female-dominated culture that seeks to resolve conflicts by talking, not by right and by strength, we have no more desire to defend women. Why would we, having been insulted and called "misogynist pigs," and so on, for decades? What advantage would accrue to us from protecting you? If, despite all of our efforts, nothing that we do is good enough for you... go ahead and manage on your own!

This is one of the symptoms of the death of a tribe, a people, a civilization... because on the other side of the wall—and already numbering in the millions in our cities—there are other tribes, peoples and civilizations, thanks to galloping population growth, and they are just waiting for the right moment to replace us, demographically and culturally, if not through our outright extermination. Among these peoples there is no sensitivity to criticism and no sense of guilt, and any discussion with loud-mouthed feminists on the usefulness or the lack thereof of a "patriarchy" is likely to be concluded by throwing stones at them.[134] Among these peoples, the feminist—even if

---

134 To be fair, the Koran does not mention stoning in any of its texts. However, Islamic law—that is to say, Sharia—quotes stoning as punishment in cases of adultery committed by a married person having had sex outside

lesbian—is married off by force, and, willingly or not, is made to produce with her womb the next generation of proselytizing and conquering warriors.

Now do you get it?

But then some men will rebel and follow their instincts, and will protect you no matter what... in the face of a hostile media, politicians, and even the law.

Other men will go away (mentally or physically) and create new tribes, or join other tribes—ones that are more accepting of their instinctual self, and where they can find their eternal virtues of strength, courage, mastery and honor.[135]

But their number is tiny, and most men in the "Western tribe" aren't interested in protecting women. The achievements of the "century of women" that I have described in this book may not last. And the civilization which, alone among all those anywhere around world, was able to create the conditions for freedom of thought and action, and to make freedom possible for women, may disappear.

Really, the choice is yours.

It is your choice because most men are programmed to please you in hopes of getting to have sex. We are ready to do anything, even to love you, obviously even to submit to your

---

marriage with penetration if and only if four witnesses clearly saw penetration. Unless it is an orgy, which is rare in Muslim countries, or sex in public, it is impossible for sex with penetration to be observed by four people. Nonetheless, death by stoning is practiced in countries where Sharia is law: Afghanistan, Saudi Arabia, UAE, Iran, Nigeria, Pakistan, Sudan and Yemen. Coming soon to Europe and America?

135 See *The Way of Men* by Jack Donovan,
http://www.jackdonovan.com/axis/what-is-masculinity/

most humiliating[136] orders. If your wish us to once again become strong, brave, just and protective, then we will. So it is up to you, ladies, to prove to us that not only will you always want us to take part in your life, but that you admire us for the virtues that make us who we are.

It's a question of your survival.

---

136 Unless the local culture is such that we can take what we want by force, which is the one thing that Western cultures, since the middle ages and the advent of "amour courtois," has made unacceptable.

Acknowledgements

It isn't a simple matter for a man to write a book about women. On the one hand, there is a secret in women, which they safeguard jealously, in order to keep us in ignorance. On the other hand, in a certain social environment, whose representatives call themselves survivalists, there are misogynistic stereotypes. It's no accident that there is a joke: "In case of catastrophe, women and children are evacuated first, to allow us to then calmly look for solutions." No matter how deep my respect for women, I am not insured against similar inadvertent insults, even if they are made in jest.

I want to express my deep gratitude to all the women who helped me to better understand the fragility of personality and the psychological and anthropological functioning of half of humanity: my wife, who has been a my indefatigable supporter during the 12 difficult months during which this book was born; my two daughters, who demonstrated their intelligence, creativity and even their feminine guiles; my mother, who always believed in me—how crazy is that?—in everything I do, and thanks to whom I, upon becoming a husband and the father of four children, began to understand what a mother is able to give to her children; to the first readers of this manuscript, thanks to whose harsh but fair criticisms I hope to have been able to avoid generalizations and hackneyed sexist stereotypes.

With profound gratitude I would like to thank all the women I have interviewed in many parts of the world, and who generously shared with me their experience in achieving autonomy. You are amazing! Keep it up!

I would also like to thank Claire Severac for her foreword and advice. But most importantly I would like to thank my friend Vol West, who made a huge contribution to this book: fleshing it out, making corrections, giving advice and harsh but fair criticism...

I would also like to thank you, my readers, for reading my book all the way through, for supporting me in carrying out this project and have introduced your tender feminine presence into a world of boorish boors. We, men, count on you from the bottoms of our souls, and want you to help us, support us, love us and allow us to love you in our own way, which is sometimes very different from the way you love, and that we, upon becoming more mature in our relationships, could accomplish great things... together.

40562288R00156

Made in the USA
Middletown, DE
16 February 2017